The Battle
of Jefferson
Canyon

To R.J. Smith

Don Bowman

First Edition: Published by Spur, Inc. May 1996
Back cover photo by Don Bowman
Cover design and art by Shyla Cook

Typeset in Times New Roman by Spur, Inc.
2040 Reno Hwy #2, Fallon, Nevada 89406
Fallon, Nevada 89406
Telephone 702/423-6197, Fax 702/428-1524

Printed by Griffin Printing, 4141 North Freeway Blvd.,
Sacramento, California 95834. 916/6493511
Telephone (916)649-3511

Bowman, Don, 1937
      The Battle of Jefferson Canyon
    and other skirmishes in the War on the West--1st edition

Includes index

    ISBN 0-9652738-0-6

    Library of Congress Catalog Number 96-92273

ACKNOWLEDGEMENTS

I am extremely grateful for the assistance of the many people who made this book possible. Without their help, this book would have had a much narrower field of view. I hope the end result will be worthy of their time and effort. Many unnamed people have also contributed to this undertaking. I sincerely thank everyone for their help, especially the following list of friends and supporters:

Lee Pitts....Morro Bay, CA, for spurring me into writing and for his contributions to this book.

Michon Mackedon....Fallon, Nevada, for her editing skills and patience

Zane Miles .... Eureka, Nevada and

Mike Mackedon.....Fallon, Nevada, For their time spent honing my legal understanding.

Brandy Bowman.... Fallon, Nevada for her help with research and for support.

Linda Stephens.......Fallon, Nevada

Kieth Lancaster....Fallon, Nevada

Tim Walters.........Safford, Arizona

Diana Dearen.... Fallon, Nevada

Howard Hutchinson... Glenwood, New Mexico

Kaye Bowman....Fallon, Nevada

Chuck Stocks....Albuquerque, New Mexico

Ruth Kaiser.....Bountiful, Utah

THIS BOOK IS DEDICATED TO THE

PEOPLE AND THE LEADERS

WHO HAVE THE GUTS

TO TRY TO DO WHAT IS

RIGHT............ REGARDLESS OF THE

POLITICAL TIDES OF THE TIMES.

CONTENTS

THE SPARK

Richard Carver was boiling mad. Sweat was running down his forehead and dripping into his eyes as he stared across the glaring expanse of the high desert valley that had been his home since he was born. He had been muscling a load of hay onto a truck, preparing to feed some livestock, when someone told him Bob Wilson had just been arrested.

Bob Wilson was an excellent mechanic, a semi-successful miner, a great helper of the unfortunate, and Carver's childhood mentor. He had taught the young lad how to get by in the great "outback" of the western U.S. with ingenious use of whatever was at hand-- Valuable information when you are 18O miles from any decent selection of services or commodities.

Well into his sixties, Bob was arrested by the U.S. Forest Service and U.S. Marshall for repairing the road into his own mining claim, a road which had been in existence for more than a hundred years. The mine he had acquired several years before consisted of underground tunnels and a unique mill site with a water-wheel driven ball mill. It was located midway up South Twin River in the Toiyabe Range, Nye County, Central Nevada. The Forest Service would not issue Bob a maintenance permit for the washed out road, so he just proceeded to fix it anyway. Now he was on his way to the federal lock up in Las Vegas.

Carver kicks a hay bale and cusses, "Sonsabitches." He cannot understand why anyone would want to harass that old man. He thinks to himself that the regulators are getting completely out of hand and somebody ought to do *something.* "Here I'm a county commissioner and can't do a damn thing about it," he ponders and mumbles some more.

Carver's friends had plied him with drinks at an Elks Lodge crab crack a couple of years before and wheedled him into running for county commissioner. No one in the crowd knew that the man they elected would one day be rattling the cages of the federal bureaucrats like they hadn't been shaken in a long time.

Carver was instilled with the work ethic. He was a high school graduate, whose only political background was in the high school offices of the Future Farmers of America, and he did not know the meaning of the word quit.

"Maybe I can do something," he reasons and stomps off to his house to make a couple of calls. The coals are beginning to glow in what would turn into one of the biggest range wars in history.

THE BATTLELINES FORM

The Federal presence in the Western states has always been an irritation because it is felt in a major portion of the industries operating there. In some states, the federal bureaucracies had been causing consternation and concern almost from the beginning of statehood. Some state legislators say that the Western states never really achieved statehood because sovereignty was never relinquished to the states in the West, as defined by the U.S. Constitution.

Over the years, the federal agencies slowly took it upon themselves to gather up more country, assert more authority, and demand more obedience. They managed to get by with their program, as long as they established their agenda, a bit at a time. The people who were being dictated to whined and howled, but reluctantly submitted time and again. There were negotiations, periodically. However, on almost every occasion the people traded for a loss.

With the advent of the Clinton Administration, the irritating federal rash became a major case of shingles, Even though the president is elected, his appointees and their legions of hired underlings operate more like a monarchy, answering to no one but themselves. Any sort of effort to bring relief from bureaucratic regulation is always a drain on finances and time and almost always futile.

President Clinton and Vice President Gore have always been avowed environmentalists, with no workable knowledge of the West. Following the 1992 election, they were out to save the countryside, no matter what it cost the rural economies. The two were present for timber hearings in the Northwest, making a huge show of concern for the families thrown out of work by their actions. A film called *California's Changing Forest,* produced by Earth Vision Institute and marketed by California Forestry Association, showed Clinton promising a little girl that her family will be taken care of through federal programs and education, replacing the lost income derived from harvesting the forest.

Ironically, as the film continues, the little girl was interviewed again a year later and she said that nothing had been done to help her family or the town, which was now half boarded up and almost closed. Her family was destitute, unable to afford even a few of the small extras of life, like a pizza or a movie once a month. Clinton's promises were merely political lip service.

The film also documents how huge forest fires have destroyed thousands of board feet of usable timber. Money that should be going to loggers, manufacturers, retailers, dispersing out through the local economies was going up in smoke needlessly. The American taxpayers were footing the bill to pay federal fire fighters to maintain a sicker and sicker forest. Scientists and forest management experts were becoming alarmed and fearful of the eventual complete degradation of forest resources. Thousands of board feet of timber were being wasted, left to disease, insects and fire in a downward spiral of forest decay.

Exploring a similar point, Dr. Alston Chase, renowned scientist, wrote *Playing God in Yellowstone,* which is now a textbook at Harvard, Yale and other schools. The book tells how the fallacies of federal management ideas like those of Clinton and Gore have degraded the true historic trends of nature and consequently harmed this huge National Park. The same things were happening everywhere as management plans, based on politically correct, abstract and unfounded ideals rather than science, upset nature and people dependent on nature.

By 1995 many people were saying the states were so overpowered by federal laws and rules that there was hardly any state sovereignty left. As a result, statehood had been reduced to the status of a colony in many respects. The people living in these western colonies and many of their legislators, like Dick Carver, were beginning to resist the accelerating domination by the federal government, a resistance which has earned the title the "County Movement."

People who opposed the County Movement were fearful of being locked out of the public lands by ranchers, loggers miners and other private users. But they are being locked out now by their own government. During the previous few years, the federal government had put up "No Trespassing" signs, restricting vehicular access and locking most of the general public out of huge tracts of range land through wilderness designations, road closures, and local

The Battle of Jefferson Canyon

policy some federal managers saw fit to make. These lockouts have not only stultified ranching, but drastically reduced enjoyment and use of the public lands by most people. These lockouts were made without consulting local elected officials, who have been protesting vigorously in meetings with federal land managers.

Bruce Babbitt, upon garnering the Secretary of the Interior post, was not content to continue the slow mode of taking more power. He took a running start and with one violent shove stirred up a rebellion, the likes of which had never been seen before, over what many would consider small issues. He and his counterparts in the United States Forest Service could have continued slowly and probably gotten by with it, but their impatience was to be their nemesis.

Nye County Commissioner, Dick Carver usually thanks Bill Clinton and Bruce Babbitt, somewhere in his speeches, for waking everyone up. The Clinton Administration's actions mobilized an opposing army in the sagebrush, which was waging a counterattack without guns. Clinton's War on the West as it was called, was going to bring no easy victory. No sooner than one box of legal rocks was thrown at the feds, than another box of a different color would be found and be used as additional ammunition.

This book is not about solutions, which may be a long time coming. This story is about the problems and the efforts being made to address those problems. The Battle of Jefferson Canyon was the major turning point. This confrontation, even though it was sometimes labeled as an illegal defiance of government, was actually an orchestrated act of civil disobedience. This one conflict was to become the center piece for the County Movement and the motivation for the people of the west to stand up and fight. This fight could have been fought with guns but, thank God, it was not.

The war was not just over natural resource management but about local government's ability to function properly on the issues directly affecting their people. The federal government was not only taking away the power of local government but also taking private property rights without compensation.

The people of the West were armed with only the Constitution and very limited funds, while the federal government was armed with massive resources of manpower and money. It was a lopsided fight, but most battles with government are.

A few really atrocious actions by federal employees, even though they are not common place, can incite some serious resolution in people desiring change.

The Battle of Jefferson Canyon

THE TREE POLICE

Incidents perpetrated by the U.S. Forest Service and BLM, like the arrest of Bob Wilson, had become more and more bizarre over the years. First off, only the FBI and the Secret Service have warrantless arrest authority in some states. According to the Constitution, police powers on federal property have to be ceded to the federal government by the state. Some say that power can only be ceded on federal enclaves (forts, dockyards, stockades and needful buildings). In any case the Nevada Legislature did not see fit to allow even the Federal Marshall's request for arrest authority in 1993.

How then, did the U.S. Forest Service confiscate Wayne Hage's cattle in 1991 without a court order? Wayne Hage had previously written a book, *Storm Over Rangelands*, which had taken the federal land management agencies to task. Hage, in the early seventies, could see the federal takeover coming and tried to wake the ranching community up. Wayne's well-annotated book is a treatise on the history of the rangelands and the split estate of rights to graze, mine, and other rights on the rangelands. Wayne contended the split estate had been established by years of prior use of the rangelands. The confiscation of Hage's cattle was for trespass and degradation of resources. Hage had pictures to disprove the overgrazing allegations and said the range was property right established by his predecessors in title and essentially, not subject to trespass. Several years later, many ruefully wished they had listened to Wayne. Wayne's book talks about the split estate of grazing and other range land uses, and how the federal government was taking away property rights in connection with those uses. In the following years it looked as though the USFS had a vendetta going against Hage just because of the book.

When the cattle were confiscated, Dave Young, the same USFS special investigator who later faced Dick Carver in Jefferson Canyon, arrived with his own army of help and supervised the operation. Young then had the cattle transported without a brand inspection, a clear violation of Nevada State law and he attempted to consign the cattle for sale at Gallagher Livestock Auction, Fallon, Nevada.

Tim Gallagher asked to see a court order and all the USFS could do was produce their own paper work and quote their own regulations. Gallagher's attorney, Jim Sloan, advised Tim Gallagher that he could be held liable for assisting in a theft, if things went wrong. Tim refused to sell Hage's cattle, partly because of the liability and partly because he felt helping the Forest Service in this particular action was morally wrong.

The livestock were then trucked to a BLM wild horse facility where the herd was sold. All this was done without the Forest Service going through regular criminal or civil procedure.

The Hage Story is not the only example of outrageous and vindictive behavior by land management

The Battle of Jefferson Canyon

agents. In Utah, Book Cliff rancher, Jim Wilcox, found his cattle stranded by washed out trails in a remote area along the Green River. Some early spring storms had washed out mountain trails familiar to the cattle, preventing their return out of the canyon. Jim had told the BLM that he planned on getting the cattle out as soon as weather permitted. The terrific summer heat could kill cattle forced to climb out of the steep canyon in the summertime, and the cattle's welfare was Jim's reason for the delay. He even gave the bureau the date he planned on removing the stock. Jim planned on using another trail he had traveled on into the canyon, which the cattle had not used before.

The BLM said that there were no trails out of the canyon and the river bottom was severely over grazed. Jim said both statements were false and that the BLM knew it. Jim told them about the other trail and produced pictures proving there was abundant feed in the area. Nevertheless, the stock was declared to be in trespass by the BLM.

A group of overzealous BLM agents put into the Green River with rubber rafts and floated into the canyon where the cattle were living. They were carrying rifles and were out hunting trespassers! When the hunting party found the cattle, the canyons echoed with gunfire. After the sounds of the shots had died away, a herd of cows, calves and bulls had been slaughtered, senselessly. Seventeen cattle were not only killed without reason, but according to pictures taken and testimony by Jim, not one was shot cleanly. Calves were gut shot, cows with broken legs were left to wallow and die, crippled bulls wandered about until they collapsed. Some of the cattle floundered, digging out pits in the sand, as they struggled for hours to regain their feet, while dying slowly in the heat. It was a brutal, barbaric and inhumane afternoon.

Having solved the trespass problem, the bureaucrats then motored back up the river and loaded their rafts. Back at the office, it is rumored they bragged to fellow employees about the day's escapades, actually proud of what they had done. The cattle in the canyon were slowly dying, while the exultant men boasted of their shooting skills.

The agents had taken on the role of judge and jury in an action that just deserved a bit of rational thought. Is this the way responsible people deal with everyday problems?

Why were land management agencies suddenly giving employees badges and guns, then telling them they were to enforce the law? A cabin on a patented mining claim in San Juan Canyon, Nye County, Nevada was burned to the ground and USFS employees were the only people seen leaving the canyon on snowmobiles shortly afterward. Roads used for years were closed for wilderness study, wildlife protection, etc.

In 1994 The BLM issued a statement saying photographers had to pay a fee if they took pictures of the public lands and sold them for profit. Now,

The Battle of Jefferson Canyon

EVERYBODY was being locked out of the public lands, unless you were a federal employee. Whose land is this anyway? Isn't this equivalent to charging a fee to take pictures of the county courthouse?

The Tree Police, was the title of a story by Lee Pitts in the September 12, 1994 issue of the *Livestock Market Digest*, exposing <u>yet another</u> abuse of federal power. Lee is a very thorough and credible writer. One thing he hasn't had to do is apologize for having the facts wrong. Here is the most bizarre story of federal misuse of power researched and written by Lee Pitts:

> You can't tell a New Mexican family that all the Bureau of Land Management does is to look after the welfare of our federal lands. In July of this year BLM Rangers allegedly shot out their car's tire, maced the driver twice, kicked one woman, stomped another and broke her ankle and told the other family members they would have their heads blown off. What was this family doing wrong you may ask? Who knows? The BLM Rangers to this day have failed to file any charges.

> Unbelievable? Not really. It is just one of the growing number of incredible incidents involving agencies of Bruce Babbitt's Interior Department. On July 24 of this year a New Mexican family was on a

family outing to the Santa Cruz Lake area in the northern part of the state. After fishing and picnicking for two hours, the family loaded up their car and were leaving the area when they were stopped by a BLM Ranger. According to a complaint filed by the family's attorney, the BLM Ranger approached the vehicle carrying a shotgun and ordered everyone out of the car using threats of bodily harm laced with profanity. The BLM Ranger fired his shotgun at the car to show that he meant business.

The complaint continues: Three men got out of the car and asked why they were being stopped. They asked if it was for fishing without a license, but they were never asked for their fishing licenses. When one man and the women and children tried to leave, the BLM Ranger shot out the car's tire and the driver got out of the disabled car with his hands outreached to be handcuffed. It is alleged that the BLM Ranger then maced the driver and handcuffed him. The driver's girlfriend, who was also handcuffed, tried to help the driver by licking the mace off his eyes and was kicked twice by the BLM Ranger to stop her from helping the driver. The driver's mother tried to help her son but was knocked to the ground by the ranger who then stomped on her leg before handcuffing her. After handcuffing the mother the BLM Ranger went back to the driver and sprayed him again in the face with mace. All this time the children were crying and the ranger yelled at them to shut up. According to the complaint the BLM Ranger said he was going to blow their (expletive deleted) heads off. Only the timely arrival of

The Battle of Jefferson Canyon

a deputy sheriff and a tribal police officer may have kept the rangers from brutalizing the family further.

It gets worse. When one of the men picked up one of the children to comfort him, the BLM Ranger put his shotgun to the child's head and ordered the man to put the child down. Two other BLM Rangers allegedly arrived and began waving their weapons around as well. The BLM Rangers refused to call an ambulance for the lady who has suffered a broken ankle and the BLM Rangers refused to say why they had stopped the family in the first place. The adults were incarcerated and the BLM Ranger did not notify the Attorney General as they were required to do. Although records at the Santa Fe jail indicate six adults were arrested on charges of assault and hindering a federal employee, a U.S. magistrate released all those jailed because the BLM did not produce a written complaint and no formal charges were made. To this day the family still has no idea why they were arrested.

Remember these are federal land management employees, who are initiating these atrocious acts. It is not the Federal Bureau of Investigation, nor the Bureau of Alcohol Tobacco and Firearms, or any other law enforcement agency.

The power hungry bureaucracies have designated themselves police powers, without having proper authority or training. The agents are turning into bullies with little respect for people or property.

Lee's article was definitely the epitome of a burecracy gone haywire. It was mobilizing the troops from the grass roots.

The Battle of Jefferson Canyon

CARVER GETS THE WORD

Wayne Hage told Dick Carver in 1989 that there was a person that he should meet. Hage had been involved with setting up the National Federal Lands Council, where he had become acquainted with Ed Presley. Somewhere in the year of 1992, Russ Fields from the Nevada State Department of Minerals called Dick to inform him that there was a fellow scheduled to speak in Yerington, Nevada that he thought Carver would be interested in hearing.

It turned out to be Ed Presley, who was giving a seminar on misuse of authority by federal agents and employees. Presley maintained that in many cases the federal agents had drastically overstepped their bounds, both knowingly and based on many preestablished misconceptions. He gave case histories and supportive evidence of federal abuses and how they were dealt with in some instances. Presley was a researcher for attorneys on federal cases and had much experience filing Freedom of Information Act (FOIA) requests. Ed had worked mostly on actions involving the Internal Revenue Service.

Carver made a special trip to hear the talk, and said, "I haven't ever been the same since." The commissioner found out that many times federal employees were operating outside their delegated authority and beyond their Constitutional jurisdiction. Carver then started wondering about the legal jurisdiction of the employees of the federal land management agencies: the U.S. Forest Service (USFS) and the Bureau of Land Management (BLM).

In 1993, Wayne Hage's daughter, who was working for the Nevada Mining Association, alerted Dick to the fact that the U.S. Marshall's office was petitioning the Nevada Legislature for arrest authority in the state.

Dick called me and asked for assistance in defeating the bill. I said, "Hell, they already have arrest authority, don't they?" Dick said, "If they have it, why are they asking for it?"

I thought Dick had been eating loco weed. I wouldn't go along with such a radical proposal even if it meant a trip of only sixty miles.

To prepare a case against the bill, Dick and Ed Presley made many copies of *Jurisdiction Over Federal Areas Within the States.* Sometimes called the Eisenhower Report, it had been developed by the Attorney General of the United States in 1956 and discussed the limitation of arrest authority of federal agents within states. They rushed to the legislative hearings, pushed a market basket full of the copies through the halls and delivered a copy to every legislator. (This turned out to be a waste of time because most of the legislators never opened the document and it was information that should be required reading for all state officials)The bill they were trying to defeat had already passed the senate and was now before an assembly committee.

The Battle of Jefferson Canyon

Carver and Presley drafted a willing lobbyist in the form of Dave Horton, a Carson City attorney and former Lander County District Attorney, who years before had published a small pamphlet about the public lands. Dave was a fearsome defender of the Constitution and later became a faithful supporter of Dick Carver

The three then managed to get the bill defeated in committee, essentially stopping the matter from being brought to the floor of the Assembly.

The U.S. Marshals left the meeting seething. After making an end run around the Nevada Senate, they had thought their request would be a cinch to get past the Assembly, but an intense effort by two individuals stopped their train from leaving the station.

Dick and Ed came back through Fallon following their victory and invited me to dinner. The exuberant pair regaled me with the stories of the day's work. Dick told me he thought the Forest Service and BLM didn't have any police powers, handed me a copy of the Eisenhower Report and said, "Read this."

Carver told me that with my connections with the media (one or two agriculture publications at the time) I should write on this subject and added, "Somebody should write a book." He knew what I was going to do before I even dreamed of attempting such a task. My total experience writing consisted of writing a humor column, "Horsefeathers," for the *Nevada Rancher* publication. Up to that time I had only written one or two serious articles for publication and drafted real estate contracts on ranch properties.

Just like about everyone else who is approached on this subject, I disbelieved Carver's notion that the federal government did not have the supreme powers over the public lands. It was like being told you were adopted after you were 50 years old. I thought the federal government had unlimited power. I was convinced of this by years of watching how government operated and witnessing the immense control it had been asserting in the West.

That night I started reading the 600 page Eisenhower report on jurisdiction which was published in two parts: Part I, Facts and Committee Recommendations and Part II, Text of the Law of Legislative Jurisdiction. The more I read, the more I had to read, and at 2 o' clock in the morning, the report had convinced me that Carver and Presley were headed down a path that had merit. The arguments of jurisdiction and supremacy would abound over the next years of conflict between the feds and the local governments of the West.

Carver had Ed Presley file FOIA requests on issues in Nye County in the summer of 1993. The fire of rebellion found more fuel.

The Battle of Jefferson Canyon

Carver found someone to write the story. I have always maintained Carver couldn't find me on April Fools Day so he just celebrated a bit late at my expense. After the Battle of Jefferson Canyon I suddenly became an authority on the County Movement and several publications began to print my stories. After two years my office was a storehouse of court decisions, research papers and trash can material from the fringe element.

THE RESEARCH SOLDIERS

While Dick Carver was out expounding on statehood acts and equal footing, there was one person in the background, who spent his time reading Supreme Court decisions and digging up more ammunition for the cause. Dave Haight of Yerington, Nevada, worked countless hours with one thing in mind: find the key decisions that supported state sovereignty.

Dave was a retired electronics engineer, who did not have a law degree, although he had spent considerable time in law school. Dave reread every case used by the feds to support their hold on supremacy. He found some of the cases cited by the DOJ counsels to be completely misinterpreted. The feds had been using some of the pleadings which supported their ideas, while ignoring the findings of the courts.

Subsequently, while Carver and Ed Presley were at a cattlemen's meeting in Elko in 1993, Dave came up with one of the best cases for states' rights up to that time, *Utah vs United States*, 1992. The Lyon County District attorney had tipped Dave that there was a recent Supreme Court case having to do with equal footing. The case touched on statehood acts and jurisdiction over lands within a state.

Dave worked tirelessly, spending hours in a law library at the Capitol. He then enlisted some help from the Nevada Legislative Counsel Bureau, in the form of an ally in the Counsel Bureau whose boss also did not support the County Movement. More attorneys than not, when approached with these jurisdiction issues, automatically would say you have to be nuts to challenge the authority of the federal government which has always had supremacy. But, an attorney who is willing to listen and read almost always becomes an advocate of jurisdictional challenge.

Dave used yet another Supreme Court case to bolster the campaign, *New York vs. United States*, 1992. This case was over a nuclear dump, an issue which Nevada was currently facing on a huge scale. The findings said the federal government could not "commandeer " a state government and make it do anything. And, even if that happened, anything the state enacted under such duress was null and void. Dave found the case, and after it was publicized, it was used time and again, even by the Nevada Legislature and the State of Utah for assertion of state control.

Dave would instill in Carver, after countless sessions, the importance of equal footing, not equal footing doctrine. He claimed the equal footing doctrine had to do with political equality of the states and was developed over time. Equal footing was the state equality in every way, including acquiring all unappropriated land at the *time of statehood.* He said the main question to ask was not about present ownership of the public lands but about "title vesting at statehood." Dave claimed that if title vested at statehood, the rest of the argument was already made. He said time and again, "You have to ask the right question."

Help for the fight came from many directions. Jim Bauman of Eureka, Nevada, sent in a clipping found by the Eureka County Manager, Lennie Forenzie, who was reading old newspapers in the Eureka library. Lennie had come across an article in an 1880 paper, which told of congressional actions of the time.

The Dagget Land Bill was being discussed May 20, 1880, a portion of which allowed the State of Nevada to exchange two million acres of unmarketable school lands scattered throughout the state for public lands suitable for sale. The article said, "Mr. Dagget procured passage of the bill tonight by a weak-kneed little speech, in which he explained its necessary, and by showing among other things that the state has been thus far unable to find purchasers for more than seventy thousand acres of her school grants. He replied to objections by Sparks, of Illinois, by showing there was no danger of the state monopolizing all the best farming land, under this bill, because the land of Nevada had long ago passed out of the hands of the federal government."

The article raised some big questions. Was Dagget saying that statehood had already transferred all of the land to the state? Did the congress at the time of statehood never intend to keep any land within the Western states?

Nevada was granted statehood because of it's huge mineral resources. Money was needed to fight the Civil War. The congressional act for statehood said that the public lands *shall be sold and the funds used to pay the national debt. Five percent of such sales were to go to the State of Nevada.* This clause raised more serious questions:

The Battle of Jefferson Canyon

What if the government ended up being forced, by adhering to the statehood contract, to divest itself of the land? Was this what the people, who were trying to wrest control away from the federal government, wanted? Would the American taxpayer advocate privatization of the public land if it would reduce the national debt?

Confusing agreements had been made. The federal government had complied with Article I, sec 8, of the Constitution for years, getting state legislative approval for land acquisitions for needed federal installations. Then suddenly they stopped doing this and just took up land from their own agencies--Trust lands that were supposed to be disposed of and put on the tax rolls.

Why was long-established protocol being ignored when for years it was rigidly adhered to? The more research that was done, the more questions began to surface. How was ownership of the trust lands acquired if state legislative approval had to be adhered to for acquiring other federal lands?

These anomalies were the cause of much of the conflict that was to spring up during the ensuing years. Both the rules and the previous contracts had been ignored. Replies to the FOIA requests by Nye County showed the federal government did not really know what its true position amounted to.

Some of the first FOIA requests, concerning a few lots in the mining town, dredged up paydirt as far as Carver was concerned.

The Battle of Jefferson Canyon

PROVE IT!

In 1993, Jim Kielhack, a real estate broker, placed "for sale" signs on lots in the town of Round Mountain, Nye County, Nevada. He had acquired these lots through a tax sale from Nye County several years before. The lots had been previously traded and sold since the mining camp had been established in the 1800's. Jim and everyone who lived in the town of Round Mountain knew the town was established on top of some mining claims. Many mining towns in Nevada, Virginia City, Austin, Goldfield, Tonopah, all have similar situations.

A Bureau of Land Management Ranger wearing a badge and a gun delivered a letter from the Tonopah District manager and told Jim to take down his signs. The letter stated that the land was federal property and was not for sale or lease. The town had not been properly registered as a townsite, according to the BLM.

Remember, the BLM Ranger had no police power and he did not have a document that a sheriff would have produced in a similar situation--a court order.

When the matter was brought to County Commissioner Richard Carver, he recalled what he had learned from Ed Presley's seminar on federal jurisdiction. He asked Ed to write a Freedom of Information Act (FOIA) request to the

BLM, asking the agency for the documentation showing it owned the land and had jurisdiction over the specific parcels.

The reply came back, "We have no documentation regarding your request." Carver and Presley anticipated this kind of reply, which started a line of similar requests for the next several months. Both men believed that unless the property fell under the specific classes of land of which Constitution allows federal ownership, federal jurisdiction was nil. They continued to receive replies and the answers all read the same. It looked like Carver and Presley were on the right track.

The questions in Carver's mind were; "How could the federal government claim ownership without paying for it and getting state approval? How could the federal government claim ownership over land that did not fall within the criteria of Article I?"

Article I, section 8, clause 17 of the United States Constitution is a clause stating that congress shall have the power: To exercise exclusive Legislation in all Cases whatsoever, over all Places purchased by the *consent* of the Legislature of the State in which the same shall be, for the Erection of Forts, Magazines, Arsenals, dockyard, and other needful Buildings.

The federal government then began to say they had jurisdiction through Article IV, section 3 of the Constitution which states, "Congress shall have the power to dispose of and make needful Rules and Regulations respecting the Territory or other Property belonging to the United States."

Where is the territorial land talked about in Article IV? Hadn't Nevada achieved statehood?

These questions had been asked before by Judge Clel Georgetta, former Governor of the State of Nevada, who had gone through the whole scenario in his book, *The Golden Fleece of Nevada*. This book, published in 1972, was a historic documentation of the federal expansion of power in Nevada. Bert Smith, a cattle and sheep rancher, collared Carver at a Nevada Cattlemen's Convention, pointed to *The Golden Fleece* on a table of books and said, "You should read this." Carver read that book at least three times, while referring to a pocket copy of the Constitution that had taken up permanent residence in his shirt pocket.

Here Carver stood with a rule book in his pocket that nobody was adhering to. A game was being played by a team that was changing the rules, just because they were bigger and more powerful. These were the very actions that drafters of the Constitution were fearful of and tried to address in their well-thought out document. It was time to drag out the rule book and yell, "Foul."

THE CARVER LETTER

Dick Carver mulled over the replies made by the feds to his FOIA requests, which offered no proof of federal ownership. He worried about what was happening to the rights of the states and their citizens. He wanted to write a letter to the Secretary of the Interior that would force an answer on jurisdiction of the public lands. He decided that he didn't know enough to write the letter, unassisted so he asked for help.

Carver asked Ed Presley to help him draft a letter. Presley told Dick to write the letter himself, because he knew enough to get the point across. Carver read and reread Supreme Court decisions, Clel Georgetta's book, the *Golden Fleece of Nevada* and the U.S. Constitution and began drafting the letter. In the end, the original letter expanded from 3 or 4 pages to 28 pages of assertions and citations from court cases.

The farther Dick read, the more he believed that the Federal agencies had been operating out of bounds. He awoke at night worried about sending a letter which might make a fool of him or Nye County. Dick said, "One night I woke up and it was just like someone had turned on the light. I figured I had nothing to worry about. We had a Constitution and it was clearly behind me."

The Battle of Jefferson Canyon

He now believed that under "equal footing," the unappropriated lands passed to the state at statehood, wiping out territorial jurisdiction. "Nevada owns all public lands," was his conclusion. The letter was dated November 5, 1993.

Carver addressed the letter to the Secretary of the Interior and sent copies to Nevada Governor Bob Miller, Mike Espy, Secretary of Agriculture, plus about 50 other parties that he figured should know the facts. Bruce Babbitt, who he knew on a first name basis, was his prime target, because of a past association. Bruce had worked as a private attorney for Nye County a couple of years before. At that time, Nye County was protesting applications for water by the city of Las Vegas and hired Babbitt to represent the county. Dick says, "I want to thank Bruce Babbitt for teaching me one thing, 'Never, ever give up, when you know you are right.'"

Dick was convinced he was right. The Constitution was not that hard to read but had been interpreted to align with political views more than once.

Carver sent the letter and suddenly stepped from obscurity into the spotlight. Now called the Carver Letter, it became one of the most copied documents in history. People from all over the West who had copies turned right around and made more copies. Carver said he had been in some places where the letter had been recopied so many times, it was almost illegible. Requests for copies poured in, marking the beginning of thousands of phone calls to Nye County over the next couple of years.

Met Johnson, Utah legislator said the Carver letter had created big excitement, especially in Wyoming, and stated that he would gather all the support he could for the Nevada Movement. He said that his copy machine had been running to the max to provide copies of the Carver Letter for influential people who could lend their support. He said that the rest of the Western States could not afford to let Nevada fail.

Dick thought he would get a reply from Babbitt and for the next year defended the man against anyone who cussed him. Carver said Babbitt was a smart man and would be willing to listen to the problems presented. He did not know that when Babbitt ran for president, the environmental movement had contributed large sums to his election effort. The "Greenies," as they are sometimes called, had the clout to deafen the Secretary to the rural people's voice and states' rights. Politics were bigger than past friendships and associations. Carver was dead wrong about Babbitt being willing to listen, but his pen started to attract some attention.

Many people believed that if the Secretary of the Interior had come West at that time with something besides his lopsided Rangeland Reform, he may have defused the whole ticking bomb of revolt with a little diplomacy and compromise. But Babbitt didn't even have courtesy to reply

The Battle of Jefferson Canyon

to Carver's request. He ignored Carver and thousands of other good, hard working people while destroying businesses, jobs, and dreams.

Carver said that when he happened to be at a meeting where Congresswoman Barbara Vucanovich was speaking, he asked her if she had received a copy of his letter. According to Carver, Vucanovich said that she had the letter and that the document had created a big stir everywhere, including Capitol Hill.

At the time Dick drafted the Carver letter, it was a touch on the radical side to be quoting the U.S. Constitution. Anyone who started espousing the document in those days was treated like a religious fanatic. Carver's moves were timely, however, and by 1995 many members of congress were beginning to insert the Constitution into their political vocabulary. People tired of federal pressures were looking to the Constitution for relief. A lot of them were awakened by the Carver Letter.

However, the letter did not awaken a response from the person to whom it was initially addressed, Bruce Babbitt.

THE SILENT SECRETARY

When President Clinton appointed Bruce Babbitt as Secretary of the Interior some people jumped to conclusions. Many people in the West were relieved to hear that a person from the West, who supposedly understood ranching, timber, and mining would be running the nation's largest land management agency. It was thought that Babbitt would be able to do a knowledgeable job, uninfluenced by urban misconceptions and pressures. How wrong they were.

Bruce Babbitt, the main target of the Carver Letter, had found his way to Washington D.C. from Flagstaff, Arizona. He was the heir of a family that had struggled to build a fortune in the inhospitable high desert of the Southwest. Babbitt is the offspring of one of the most noted families of Arizona. The Babbitt clan had operated numerous business ventures in the northern part of the state for decades. There were many signs with the Babbitt name on them.....Indian trading posts, Thriftway Markets, Babbitt Department Stores, lumber yards, automobile agencies, sheep and cattle ranches. Babbitt Ranches was one of the finest livestock companies in the West. The operation owned thousands of acres of deeded land, but also grazed on public lands, primarily checkerboarded within the private land. The ranches were-well run and respected by almost everyone in Northern Arizona. The family was respected as well and treated their help and neighbors fairly.

The ranch business, risky in the best of times, was no different for the Babbitts. Babbitt ranches almost went

The Battle of Jefferson Canyon

under on three different occasions, a fact that Bruce seemed to ignore. Had Bruce taken some interest in the ranching operation, he might have learned the practical side of working with nature. He missed a great opportunity to have a positive influence on ranching and the environment.

Although Bruce Babbitt was a former governor of Arizona, he had exerted so much pressure on his home state that most of the leaders were almost livid when they spoke of him. It seems he had been snubbing his home state and his heritage.

Robert A. McConnell former Assistant Attorney General, U.S. Dept. of Justice, like most of the people at the 1994 Western States Summit II in Phoenix, Arizona, did not speak very highly of Bruce Babbitt. He quoted Senator Wallop at a Senate funding hearing with Babbitt, "Bruce, you were before this committee last year to confirm your appointment as Secretary of the Interior. You had to divest your interests and your heir's interest in the Babbitt ranch holdings and it didn't seem to bother you. It bothered me. Now, I see that it was a wise move on your part, because now you have devalued the assets drastically after you bailed out."

Governor Symington attended a Rangeland Reform meeting in Flagstaff earlier in the 1994, uninvited by the Secretary, it was rumored. The governor stood up and told

Babbitt from the audience, "The state of Arizona leases grazing for 20 per cent less that the federal government charges, and we still make a profit over management costs. The very best thing you could do would be turn the rest of the land over to the state to manage."

President Clinton may have been influenced by his wife, Hillary when he appointed Babbitt to a cabinet post, according to some people. During a Western States Summit meeting in New Mexico, a speaker revealed that Babbitt had worked as an attorney for the Navajo tribe when fresh out of law school, alongside the person who was now first lady. Evidently the political influence ran deep because about a year after his cabinet appointment, Babbitt was a candidate for a seat on the Supreme Court. A huge telephone campaign against his nomination was waged on the White House, led by Utah State Representative Met Johnson and his Western States Coalition. The telephones to the presidential offices were tied up for 3 days.

Clinton decided it was easier to nominate someone less controversial.

Bruce Babbitt, as Secretary of the Interior, sided with the environmental movement, which contributed greatly to Babbitt's failed presidential campaign. Babbitt cranked up to put an end to "welfare ranching," as reiterated time by the misinformed press. There was a move to "drag the ranching community kicking and screaming into the twentieth century."

The Battle of Jefferson Canyon

The Secretary came to Reno in early in 1994, along with Assistant Secretary Bob Armstrong, stumping for Rangeland Reform. The meetings were closed to the general public and the ranchers, who were the most affected by the reform, had the least representation.

He said that former Interior Secretary, Harold Ickes, was his hero and that he was going to emulate his philosophies. Harold Ickes was Interior Secretary when the Taylor Grazing Act was implemented. The grazing act had been called for by distressed ranchers across the West, who were fighting over grazing rights and wanted the range wars to cease. Ickes may have taken the credit for a tremendous job, but the man who really did the work was Farrington Carpenter, a Colorado rancher and attorney who helped draft the original legislation. Ickes promptly started bending Carpenter's work out of shape, desiring monarch-like power for his post.

Ickes appointed Carpenter to implement the act and gave Farrington a budget of $140,000 and the assistance of seventeen technicians from the U.S. Geological Survey. No one knew how big the public domain was or where it was located. Ferry Carpenter had the maps made and adjudicated the range in one year!

Ferry did not have the manpower to do the job, so he accomplished this amazing feat with volunteer help. The only expedient way to do this he reasoned, was to turn the job over to the stockmen themselves.

The basic rules were: the range was to be apportioned on the basis of prior use, by people who owned private land in the vicinity; the range was to be divided into districts and a federal grazier (referee) was to be put in charge of each district; these were then to be the adjudicated grazing rights to the forage on the public domain. Rights were adjudicated based on previously established possessory interests in the rangeland.

Ferry had no intention of creating a vast bureaucratic complex occupying thousands of offices and eating up the taxpayer's money. He had established a self-regulating operation that required minimal supervision. He turned back $60,000 of the $140,000 budgeted to the treasury! His Washington counterparts hated him. They said it was no way to run a bureaucracy. Even Carpenter's boss, Harold Ickes tried to get him fired. But Carpenter would make a few phone calls and manage to retain the job. He didn't turn loose of the post until he was sure the grazing boards had control and the federal intervention was minimal.

Maybe what Babbitt admired about Harold Ickes was Icke's desire to fire Carpenter, a man who knew how to get things done without spending a lot of money.

Now Babbitt was bringing forward new advisory boards, loaded with people from the environmental movement, with a small voice from local elected officials. Elected officials represented everybody, from environmentalists to resource users, so why not appoint them?

While trying to push the reform package in Reno Babbitt said, "My faith is in Jeffersonian principles." He had evidently studied a different set of history books than most people, because everyone knows Jefferson did not believe in an all-powerful federal government. In fact Jefferson did everything in his power to insure that actions like those the Secretary was now trying to implement, would be against the law. Bruce then rectified this statement by saying, "When the (local) committee delivers its findings, Billy Templeton (State BLM Director) has the final say."

Babbitt then asked questions about Nevada Water Law. When he heard enough, he said, "When a permittee leaves, we want to take over his water developments and water rights on the range. Title should be vested in the United States." (Another Jeffersonian thought?)

Rose Strickland of the Sierra Club, sat with her arms crossed, visibly huffing at the thought of even minimal local control. Dean Rhoads asked her if she believed in a Democratic form of government. She thought a bit and said, "No."

This shocking statement caused a fleeting frown to cross Babbitt's face, and he said, "If we duke it out locally, we will probably make better decisions, than decisions made from afar, as in the past." Babbitt then said, "The New Jeffersonian West is in the making."

Babbitt's promises to let locals have some of the decision making were taken as lies by most of the ranching community. This fact was exemplified by one rancher who later said, "I wouldn't trust Babbitt or Clinton in an outhouse, with a muzzle on."

Dan Heinz of the American Wildlands said, "It would be impossible for the environmentalists to attend all the meetings, in these counties spread across the west." He grumbled, "We are just having hell in Utah."(Where some experimental groups were working on local committee concepts.) It looked like the environmentalists were not as committed as they claimed, if they didn't want to attend meetings about the public lands. Over the next two years, enrollment in the Sierra Club and other groups started dropping and their funding began to dwindle, forcing reductions in their staffs and buildings.

In September of 1994, Bruce Babbitt appeared in an hour long special on Public Broadcasting, aired throughout the country. In that program Babbitt said, "The lights have been off in the Interior Department for a long time." He felt that several men preceding him had done very little in the way of proper management.

The Battle of Jefferson Canyon

Babbitt again compared himself with Harold Ickes, who also made many enemies and was instrumental in getting congress to confer almost godlike power on the Secretary of the Interior. Ickes put the Taylor Grazing bill before congress some four times, without a requirement for approval by the states. Congress would send it back asking the requirement be written in. Ickes finally was able to sneak his version through on the fifth try.

Many analysts, including Nevada's Clel Georgetta, said that the Taylor Grazing Act was grossly unconstitutional and needed to be challenged.

When asked about the sovereignty movement in the West, Babbitt scoffed, "It is a weak effort and it will get no farther than the movements before it." However, a leak out of the Forest Service had revealed that this issue was a top priority with the USFS and the BLM. The question was whether Babbitt was telling the truth and ignoring the issue, or trying to hide the fact that attorneys of the agencies were scrambling to find federal footing.

The television interviewer asked Babbitt if he were still governor of Arizona, would he not be in the forefront of the battle for state control? He replied that even as governor he backed federalism.

Richard Carver believed Babbitt was eyeing the presidency or a federal post even at that time, saying, "His ideals must have paid off, because he now has a lot better job than being governor."

For whatever reasons, Bruce Babbitt ignored the Carver Letter and a subsequent letter from Carver asking for a meeting. He scoffed at state sovereignty, turned a deaf ear to ranching families' cries of anguish, and ignored counties' economic problems, while trying to install a management plan based on abstract ideas instead of good science.

The Battle of Jefferson Canyon

NACO ENDORSES STAND

Babbitt's refusal to answer the Carver letter left Carver stewing for three months. Well, maybe Babbitt could ignore a letter from one lone county commissioner, but he would have a hard time ignoring every county in the state.

Carver had the support of the rural counties of Nevada so he pressed for support from the other counties. The annual meeting of all the Nevada counties was the place to press the issue.

The Nevada Association of Counties held its annual meeting in January of '94 in Reno. This meeting had more spectators than any previous meeting because the word was out that Carver was going to ask for endorsement on the public lands issue.

The board had invited the USFS and BLM attorneys to speak at the meeting and ruled that Carver and the attorneys would be given thirty minutes each for their presentations. Carver said he had a few house cleaning chores to go through before he could begin. He cited federal cases that show federal employees not under oath should be presumed to be lying, according to evidence presented to the courts. Carver asked that he and the consul for the government be placed under oath by the Lander County Clerk.

Jim Stringer, from the Department of Agriculture (USFS) objected vehemently, "I was invited here to speak and I am not going under oath." You could almost see the hair stand up on the back of his neck. The crowd and the commissioners all roared with laughter. Counsel for the BLM concurred that he, also, would refuse to take the oath.

Carver grinned and said, "Well, I guess we will proceed without that."

A reply to the Carver Letter had been received from the USFS. "In their cites," Carver said, "they have given us the strongest case yet to support our views." The eyes of the attorneys for the government widened at this statement.

Jim Stringer in addressing the group said, "The federal government owns the federal lands and it is going to manage them." (I was later put on track by Jerry Urillo and Ed Presley that this was a correct statement. The fact that the feds can manage federal property is undisputed. Just what status the property truly possesses is in dispute.) Jim said the main goal was to encourage cooperation and resolve controversy. He brought out the point about the huge cost of ligation which the counties could not afford to fund. He also said it would be a losing battle for the counties.

Discussion followed, and Carver showed how he had gained evidence from the federal government through FOIA requests.

The Battle of Jefferson Canyon

He said the feds could not produce evidence showing they had either jurisdiction or ownership of lands designated in the requests.

Concern was expressed about counties losing federal funds, mainly payment in lieu of taxes money (PILT funds) the counties had been receiving for the federal hold on the public lands. These funds were supposed to compensate for taxes that the lands would have generated, had they been on the property tax rolls of the counties.

This concern was addressed by Eve Culverwell, a fiery little commissioner from Lincoln County, who said, "We are talking about basic freedoms. I can tell you one horror story after another about federal agents and county mandates. We are going into a black hole of economic depression. We cannot trade our economy for a federal welfare check."

The issue was highly supported by Esmerelda County Commissioner Wade Barton, who said, "After working on the advisory task force on public lands and going over research done in this effort, I have to stand with Dick. We must start demanding our constitutional rights."

The Mayor of Carson City, who headed the City-County Government in that area said, "I do not have a dog in this hunt. We have no federal lands in my county, which just encompasses Carson City. This board has always considered the needs of each county with respect, giving them equal voice on this board. I would think that now is the time for all of us to make sure we support the counties who are making this effort. I would hope that we can remain as one voice which speaks in unison."

Carver and Presley had drafted a letter requesting that Bruce Babbitt come west to meet with the counties. The object of the meeting was to plan an orderly transition from federal to county control of the public lands. Dick said that if the NACO board did not endorse the letter, it would be sent anyway by the several counties backing the Nevada Plan. This caused concern among the members, as NACO had always been supportive of the rural counties' needs and they did not want a division of the group.

When the vote came down it was unanimous to send the letter to the heads of the US Forest Service and the Department of the Interior. Dick Carver jumped up hollering, "Yeah." The audience and most of the commissioners applauded and cheered.

This was the one time Nye County had the wholehearted support from the other counties. Later, some of the NACO members backpedaled and dropped away from the issue. Only Nye, Esmerelda, Lincoln, Eureka, White Pine, and Lander Counties remained in the forefront of support. But, there were individual commissioners, such as Ron Shrimp of Humboldt County , and Roberta Skelton and Royce Hackworth of Elko County, who bailed in whenever possible to back Nye County up.

The Battle of Jefferson Canyon

The letter was sent, but the leadership of NACO watered down the impact when they went to Washington, D.C. a short time later. When they met with federal officials,it is rumored, that somehow they implied the letter was no big deal.

TWO DISTRICT ATTORNEYS

Despite the early NACO support, many people disagreed with the tack the counties were sailing on. Almost everyone was of the opinion that a fight with the federal government would be a preordained loss. A lot of attorneys voiced this opinion, however, some legal heads started to read and change their minds.

The following story, written by myself, was first published August 29, 1994, in the *Livestock Market Digest*, then later in several other publications:

TWO NEVADA DISTRICT ATTORNEYS BACK THE COUNTY MOVEMENT.

Zane Miles, Lander County District Attorney and William Schaeffer of the Eureka County DA's office have written letters of opinion supporting the takeover of the public lands by the people of the state. These two men have been the only D.A.'s who have taken the time out of an already overloaded work schedule, to verify the research done by the County Movement. Both opinions are written in a straightforward manner and are easy for the average citizens to understand. And, as Grant Gerber, an Elko County attorney puts it, "If anyone doesn't believe this land issue, they just have not read far enough."

In the beginning, Zane Miles was on the opposite side of the argument. He said that Richard Carver and his

The Battle of Jefferson Canyon

crew were sailing directly into the wind and had no basis for the course they were taking. Carver loaded the attorney with his compilation of facts and asked Miles to refute his argument. A lot of attorneys won't, when confronted with this issue, dismiss it out of hand and most have egos that wouldn't allow them to admit they were wrong. Now, Zane Miles is short in stature but he showed himself to be a big man when he came back with a complete reversal of opinion. He went even farther developing a firmer foundation for the cause.

Zane Miles says that the Equal Footing Doctrine has been abused by the United States in its dealings with the public domain and the West. Citing legal and historical authorities, Zane says that the public lands in Nevada and in many other Western states are not "federal lands" owned by the federal government. According to Miles, the federal government has continued to control the public lands, but only as a trustee for the states.

The Lander DA says the United States coerced the people of the territory into an illegal act of ceding the public lands to the federal government. "The Equal Footing Doctrine has been grossly offended by federal extortion," Miles wrote.

Mile's final conclusion says, "Litigation based on the Equal Footing Doctrine to validate the claims of

Nevada and other Western states should be successful unless the U.S. Supreme Court abandons 200 years of Equal Footing Jurisprudence." Miles believes the time has come for the counties to assume control and is backing his county commission in its efforts to step into the driver's seat.

The opinion was mailed to numerous elected officials, including the Nevada Attorney General, Frankie Sue Del Papa, who had been aligning herself with the feds for quite some time now. In fact, she even helped the Forest Service prosecute Wayne Hage, when the Nevada Rancher was charged with destruction of federal property while maintaining his own ditch easement. Wayne's conviction was later overturned by the court of appeals. Nevada law clearly states that ditch rights of way are equivalent to road rights of way which can be maintained at the will of the owner. Del Papa did not defend the state law but sided with the Feds because the ditch crossed over land managed by the Forest Service. Del Papa evidently believed in federal supremacy and thought the best way to protect the environment was through the federal government, regardless of the losses of either individuals' property rights or the state sovereignty.

At a national meeting of county commissions in Las Vegas, Nevada, Zane asked a panel which included an assistant from the Nevada Attorney General's office, "Can any one of you cite a case wherein the question of ownership of the public land was raised?"

The Battle of Jefferson Canyon

Not one of the group knew of any such case.

Miles said, "The question has never been asked." He also thought it was high time the question was asked.

William Schaeffer echoes the words of Zane Miles, but adds that if many Supreme Court decisions hold true then the Nevada Attorney Generals argument "must fall." He attacked the A.G.'s informal and never published argument that the Nevada Territorial Legislature disclaimed all right and title to the public lands and showed the weaknesses of her ideas. He then laid out a trail of additional cases and told why they support the County Movement.

"To sum it up," he writes, "the emperor has no clothes and for well over a century no one has dared to say so."

Until now.....

Schaeffer's parting paragraphs contained a powerful message to the West. "After all, what is there to lose: if we follow the A.G.'s current opinion (as expressed in letters and not officially), we continue to surrender all power over public lands to the federal government; if we fight them in the courts and lose, the same thing happens -

we lose all power over the lands to the federal government. No difference."

"However, if we fight and win; they, (the feds) are GONE!"

"And, if we fight and then reach a negotiated settlement because the federal government fears we might win, then we will have at least gained something."

"Further, unlike Jeff Davis and Robert E. Lee, this states rights movement isn't going to be fought on a battlefield. And, unlike Martin Luther King Jr. and the black civil rights movement, this Western, civil rights movement isn't likely to get anyone assassinated or even beaten up. So, what's to lose by trying? Only time and money; and not much of that either when you consider what can be won; not just for Nevada and its people but also for all the Western States and their people! So why not fight?"

"Why Not?"

Unlike Miles and Schaeffer, many county attorneys have not taken time to do the research. Consequently, there is a lot of opposing force exerted by those who feel they know all about the issue without proper knowledge of constitutional powers. David Engdahl, law professor at the University of Puget Sound, says, "This is a complicated issue and hardly any colleges teach anything on the Constitution at this time." Consequently, most attorneys are not up to speed on these issues.

The Battle of Jefferson Canyon

Engdahl himself does not know if the land ownership will be decided in favor of the states but adds that even if it is not, the states still have the jurisdiction over the lands.

On July 9, 1994, the Elko County, Nevada DA, Marshall Smith, had gone so far as to advise the county commissioners of that county to disband the Public Lands Advisory Commission, saying it was ridiculous to think they could overrule the Federal Government. He further stated he would no longer provide legal assistance for the board unless the commission specifically directed him to do so.

This commissioner's meeting turned into an intense debate as the DA's office and the lands commission fought for supremacy. Tempers flared as the argument turned into a name calling, finger pointing, fist shaking, paper slamming, screaming match. The argument grew so heated that at one point, an official invited someone outside to settle the argument (meaning, in the Code of the West, with fists).

A member of the advisory board asked the commissioners why they should even listen to the D.A., because he wasn't even going to be in his office the next year. "He is leaving. We have to live with our decisions every day and we are going to do the best job we know how to do."

Finally, when the dust and smoke cleared, the commission decided to back their land board. It was the county attorney who fell in the battle. The representatives of the people of Elko County decided their constituents needed and deserved a voice on the lands.

The people of the counties in other western states are also complaining of the jealousy and single mindedness of some of their elected officials. They all talk of Elko and Nye County, Nevada and the cohesiveness of their commissions against the adversity of their local and state attorneys and their willingness to take positive, meaningful action at every opportunity. Some commissions have realized that this may be the time to fight and are beginning to work on constitutional ordinances.

Richard Carver beseeches followers everywhere, "People, don't leave the whole battle for us to fight. The issue will be decided by the force mustered at the grass roots." He urged the people of the counties everywhere to help their commissioners regain control.

Many people seem to think that this is a perfect opportunity and possibly the last chance to set the powers of government in their proper place. And, as Bill Schaeffer urges,"

Why not fight. WHY NOT?"

These were the final words of the article.

The Battle of Jefferson Canyon

Since then, Zane Miles moved to Eureka and become Deputy DA in 1995. He and Bill Schaeffer have collaborated to produce a paper called *The Equal Footing Doctrine of the United States Constitution* which addresses the Constitutional issues of public land ownership. The two have mined out more and more supportive evidence for their opinions. Even in the face of ridicule and possible defeat, they did not give up and continue to fight for county control.

WESTERN STATES SUMMIT

While the Western Counties were staging their fight to reduce Federal pressures, a much needed organization was formed for legislators of the Western States to increase their strength and get their voices heard.

The first Western States Summit was held in Denver, Colorado, on Feb. 13th and 14th, 1994. The summit was the brainchild of Met Johnson, Utah State Representative, who took on the astronomical task of putting together the historic meeting. In a thirty-day period, Met booked a meeting place, put out the agenda and managed to get an attendance of at least 150 people, including a large percentage of commissioners and legislators from the Western States.

The largest contingent was from Nevada, followed by Utah and New Mexico, which was the homeland of the "give the Feds hell" attitude. Catron County, New Mexico had developed a plan which they hoped would force federal agencies to follow their own regulations, which included county input in management decisions affecting their county. Their plan had begun to be adopted by other counties in New Mexico and Arizona.

Met had hired a professional film company to video tape the proceedings. The tape was later sent to Washington D.C. and to the media. He had previously asked everyone to submit papers on any issues affecting local and state government.

The Battle of Jefferson Canyon

Met rented a copy machine which ran steadily for two days, reproducing the papers and laying out reams of information for dissemination to the attendees.

Richard Carver and the Nevada contingent held a special information meeting on the Nevada Plan. Different from the Catron County plan, the Nevada Plan was relying on the Constitution and equal footing to gain control of the public lands. The meeting was attended by 150 people who came to hear how some Nevada counties were addressing the issue of jurisdiction over the public lands.

Carver said, "I'm in charge. It's not Bruce Babbitt whose in charge--It's me, Dick Carver." The audience laughed and gave Carver a standing ovation for his efforts to put the federal government in its proper place.

That afternoon the regular session began in a room draped with flags of the 17 western states, and after introductions, the delegation proceeded with the business at hand.

Speaker of the Utah House, Ron Bishop, gave the keynote address, saying, "We need to start challenging the federal government on the 10th amendment. (Powers not delegated to the federal government are reserved to the states and to the people). "

Bishop said he had been criticized for being too forceful and had been told, "You can collect more flies with honey than with vinegar." He grinned, "But, after all, who needs more flies."

Bill Howell, of the Southern Utah Coalition of Counties said, "We must support each other's methods to achieve the common goal for all the states." He said Summit County had asked a prestigious law firm what they thought of the Catron County ordinances. The firm said the Supreme Court had eroded the concept of the 10th amendment over time and the amendment could no longer be legally enforced. Bill said, "There is no parallel for the neutering of local government in the original 13 colonies."

If one constitutional amendment could not be enforced, what about the rest? Everyone attending was beginning to worry about the federal government ignoring state sovereignty and property rights.

Garfield County, Utah commissioner Louise Liston spoke of the endangered communities. "Most rural communities cannot have a healthy economy without relying on the public lands. The federal government is jeopardizing the future of our children by locking up our natural resources. Wise use is control of resources FOR the pubic not FROM the public. The most valuable resource is the human resource."

Dave Schweikert, Arizona House majority whip, really got everyone's attention when he told about the proposed constitutional defense fund being founded by the Arizona legislature, essentially to reestablish state sovereignty. Dave

The Battle of Jefferson Canyon

said, "We pride ourselves in Arizona, in doing everything we can to annoy the hell out of the federal government." (A stance Arizona maintained in the following years.)

Monday morning was devoted to taping a message to be carried to the President. Stakeholders (people with vested interests, who are affected by government action) beseeching the President and Congress to take the people of the west's livelihoods into consideration. (Something they had been neglecting to do.)

David Engdahl, University of Puget Sound law professor, spoke on ownership vs. governance. He said that he was very apprehensive of the ability of the states to claim ownership. He said that in any case, the jurisdiction of the public lands lies with the states. He acknowledged Ed Presley's quote of a Supreme Court judge, "Ninety percent of the attorneys in this country are incompetent." David said, "That is probably a conservative estimate."

The Nevada group asked David Engdahl and the other attorneys into the next room during a break. The debate that followed was one of the most fascinating discourses on states' rights and jurisdiction that most anyone in the group could ever expect to witness. The attorneys discussing state sovereignty seemed to be in the competent category.

David Engdahl, Ed Presley, Jerry Urillo of New Orleans, Larry Beecraft of Alabama, along with Lander County Nevada D.A. Zane Miles compared notes and argued points of constitutional law for a steady two hours. Fifty spectators from all the Western states hung onto the conversations.

The discussion ran the gamut of ownership, governance, and the trust of the public lands. The consensus of the group was that Nevada should carry the ownership issue, coupled with the doctrine that if state ownership of the lands fails, the state has jurisdiction, regardless.

Engdahl said, "God, don't rely on litigation to get what you want--you can't trust the lawyers." This was coming from a teacher who made lawyers! Engdahl is a very unassuming man. In fact, he reprimanded me for calling him "professor." He said, "It makes me look like I know more than I do." It takes an extraordinary person to make light of their position in life. David Engdahl was pleasingly self critical.

Wyoming attorney, Karen Budd, who had been helping Catron County, New Mexico in their fight to gain a foothold in Federal decision making, had the undivided attention of the audience. She told about the Boundry County, Idaho case, in which county land use ordinances were struck down in a court suit brought by a group with no standing in the issue. (A backpacker group, which had not been damaged by the ordinances.) She said it took the commissioners about 30 seconds to decide to appeal the issue.

The Battle of Jefferson Canyon

Karen said she was astounded at the turnout for the Denver meeting. She said she had expected only about 20 or 30 people, at most. She also said that every plan she had heard had merit and stated, "The plan that's going to win, is if we attack the federal government with every plan we have. Unless we get a handle on this, we are not going to have anything to leave our children."

The first Western States Summit sent everyone home with reams of information and new ideas. It was the beginning of what turned out to be a powerful nonpartisan congressional lobby. The coalition was also an organization which could exert terrific political force when called upon.

The second Western States Summit, was held May 19 and 20, 1994 in Phoenix, Arizona. Attendance doubled. Some three hundred people from several Western States, along with representatives from a few Eastern States, participated in this meeting hosted by the Arizona Legislature and Governor.

Arizona Governor Fife Symington said, "The real action in America is occurring at the state and local level. We are not here to tear government apart but to strengthen it." The Arizona legislature had approved the formation of a Constitutional Defense Council and had allotted one million dollars in funds to support the Arizona battle against the feds. The Governor urged those in attendance to take this idea home with them and emulate the program in their own states.

Symington then revealed his Arizona Land Policy 2000, along with the plans for a "super agency" to manage all the public lands in the state. He used a map of Arizona to show the overlapping jurisdictions of the various federal agencies, U.S. Park Service, U.S. Forest Service, Bureau of Land Management, Bureau of Reclamation, and U.S. Fish and Wildlife Service and referred to it as "the most bizarre land management plan ever devised." He said, "You might think the federal government, with all the people they employ, could do a good job of managing the land, but they don't. With Arizona managing its own public lands, the state could save the American taxpayer 15 million dollars per year. If the current administration wants to reinvent government, we are ready to go." Fyfe said he was sending a letter to the President, asking him to turn the lands over to the state.

Allen Freemyer, counsel to the congressional subcommittee on National Parks, Forests, and Public Lands, agreed that the federal government does not know how to conduct business. The BLM had been operating unauthorized for 10 years and the Endangered Species act was now operating unauthorized. Allen said, "The people have been screaming about subsidies for agriculture, while recreation receives 1.3 billion dollars in subsidies per year. The House of Representatives bill 4157 to turn the public lands back to the state would save the taxpayers more than one billion per year. There has been a lot of good work going on out there, concerning the equal footing doctrine

The Battle of Jefferson Canyon

and a lot of good heads are bringing points to light." He concluded that there would be some major changes in the way government works if the state movement persisted. He was right. The people kept up the pressure and elected a lot of new congressmen, who began to make life miserable for President Clinton.

Summit III in Salt Lake City, Utah and Summit IV, held in Albuquerque, New Mexico, and Summit V in Portland, Oregon continued to have good attendance. Met Johnson and Summit Co-Founder, Rob Bishop had an impressive list of coups, and Congress began to echo the cries of the coalition after each meeting. Moratoriums on rule making by agencies, revamping the Endangered Species Act, and moving toward letting the states have more control, were all ideas pursued by the forceful organization.

Met Johnson once said, "When the counties stand up and say, "That's black,' the state legislators should also stand up and say, 'That's really black."

NO SMOKEY BEAR COPS IN OUR COUNTY

As the County Movement gained momentum across the West, Nye County continued to lead the charge. The Nye County Commission, which legislates for the second largest county in the continental U.S., took a firm stance to assert its rights of jurisdiction over the public lands in Nye County.

Nye, along with several other outlying counties, had already claimed all the roads and trails within their counties as county roads and had notified the federal agencies that there would be no road closures without county permission.

On May 18, 1994, the commission issued a letter to the Law Enforcement Division of the U.S. Forest Service, notifying them of the fact that they had no jurisdiction in Nye County and that the Nye County Sheriff neither needed, nor desired the USFS's law enforcement assistance in Nye County.

On the same date the commissioners notified the BLM that should they want to post signs indicating Wilderness Study Areas along county roads, they should obtain authority from either the state legislature or the Nye County Board of Commissioners.

On May 23, 1994, the commission again asked the BLM for documentation concerning the ownership of the public lands in Nye County. The federal government had replied to this request in the past by sidestepping the question with rhetoric of federal regulations and other data but, as of that date, NOT ONE agency had stood up and said, "These lands are federal property."

In fact, during a break at the National Association of Counties meeting held in Bismark, North Dakota, Nye County Commissioner Richard Carver had a conversation with the assistant director of the Forest Service, Dave Unger. According to Carver, Unger said, "Dick, the legal beagles are having real problems with your letter." (Referring to the original letter written by Carver the previous November, addressing public land ownership).

Following through with the state ownership issue, the Nye County Commission asked the governor to deed some parcels of public land over to the county for their use. According to the Constitution, the federal government has to get legislative permission from the state to own property, and it had previously complied with this rule for acquisitions such as Hoover Dam, post offices, etc. Nevada Revised Statutes show that the White Pine County Commissioners had to approve the federal acquisition of the Lehman Caves to establish that National Monument. Nye County has asserted that if the state legislature had to give permission allowing the federal government to own land, they could surely do the same for a county.

Pam Wilcox, Nevada State Lands Registrar was asked, during a legislative committed meeting on public lands, why the federal government had been taking up land for military uses without seeking state approval, during the past several years. She said, "I don't know, they just quit doing it (seeking approval) about ten or fifteen years ago." It was time someone found out. The rule book was being ignored *again!*

The hot potato was now in the Governor's lap.

The Governor was not about to hold on to the potato, so he pitched it over the Attorney General's office. Then, Governor Miller ignored Nye County's request for deeds to public lands, saying he turned the matter over to the Attorney General for advisement. Several times after that, the central Nevada Counties asked the AG for an opinion and they were told not to expect anything along those lines from the AG. (The office ignored the counties and did not render an opinion until Nevada was later named as a defendant in the Nye County suit.)

Up to this point, the Governor of Nevada and the Attorney General had been of the opinion that the federal government owned the public lands. Could it be that after more research they might change their way of thinking? Would they continue to hold onto their opinion? Their oath of office said they must uphold the Constitution of the United States and the Constitution of the State of Nevada. Did the people who swore those oaths know what the Constitutions actually said? Few politicians or attorneys have comprehensively read the documents.

The Battle of Jefferson Canyon

There was talk of filing law suits against Federal or state public officials for failing to uphold their oath of office.

Later, Eureka County asked the Governor to merely quitclaim some public land to their county. Eureka County District Attorney, Bill Schaeffer, along with Deputy DA, Zane Miles planned on filing a quiet title action against the federal government, if the state would only release its interest. The Governor never gave the Eureka County Commissioners the time of day and would not agree to meet with them on the matter. One time he might have been available but said he had to fly to Las Vegas help to Hillary Clinton with the Democratic Party campaign. With no cooperation from the state, Eureka and Nye Counties were stymied for the time being.

Worse, the Governor had endorsed Babbitt's Rangeland Reform program, chairing the Nevada preliminary planning meetings with Bruce Babbitt on two different occasions.

The central counties of Nevada saw Rangeland Reform as an economic and environmental wreck just waiting to happen. The Department of the Interior was wanting to let the environmental community have a majority of the input on management decisions through hand picked boards.

RANGE REFORM

Nye County was doing it best to prevent Rangeland reform and disputed the idea at every opportunity. Dick Carver had been going to meetings in Oregon, New Mexico, Idaho, and Arizona. He said the economically depressed areas were really looking at the County Movement as a breath of fresh hope. Carver had been receiving a lot of heartrending letters and calls from people pleading him to continue his battle for county control.

The Department of the Interior sent out a huge document, addressing Rangeland Reform '94. Many people were studying the document and were preparing replies. When I asked Carver if he had read the EIS on rangeland reform, he replied, "Hell no, we are not going to read that thing. At the next Commissioners meeting we are going to issue a letter, stating that before we comment on any issue we want documentation that they own land, have constitutional jurisdiction, and that employees have delegated authority, and we will require an economic impact study on each issue involving the rancher and the County. We won't be allowing any range reform in Nye County."

Austin, Nevada June 8, 1994 was the site of one of the three rangeland hearings designated for Nevada. Rangeland reform hearings were all scheduled on the same day clear across the West. Just prior to the hearings in this small mountain town, county commissioners from the central counties compared notes in the latest happenings in their districts. Eureka County Commissioners, Pete Giocoechea and Leroy Etchegerry, said that the Eureka County road

The Battle of Jefferson Canyon

foreman stopped a BLM blade that was working on a road over the public land in their county. The operator was told to load up the grader and get it off the county road and that Eureka County would do its own maintenance. The machine was later found in Nye County and received the same sort of welcome.

During the hearings, Lander County Commission chairman, Ray Williams, informed those at the hearing that the BLM and Forest Service had no authority to impose national policies on the public lands. He further stated that the County expressed no opinion on the advisability of implementing rangeland reform on Lander County post office sites and that the County would not interfere in that case. He handed over a document, signed by the Lander Commissioners, verifying his statement.

Nye County commissioner, Dick Carver said, "A letter was sent to the Rangeland Reform address yesterday, informing you that Nye County does not recognize the BLM, as the land management authority for their county." And he went on to say, "Therefore as a warning to any agents, officers, or employees, imposing Rangeland Reform '94 on public lands within the borders of Nye County, that are owned by the state of Nevada, will be subject to suit for acting outside their delegated authority."

The letter further states, "Should your wish to pursue imposing Rangeland Reform '94 within areas other than the post office and the Atomic Test site in Nye County we suggest that you go to the Nevada Legislature and have other properties ceded to the federal government so that your regulations would apply."

The letter is signed by all five Nye County commissioners.

The letter was reasserted at the hearing when Carver said, Mr. Secretary, (Babbitt) AGAIN, you are not going to implement Rangeland Reform in Nye County."

Facts were compared following the hearings and in almost every hearing there was a predominance of rural people. An Interior Department Official said that when the meetings were scheduled, it was thought the environmentalists would turn out in throngs. The idea backfired. There would be 150 to 200 people speaking against reform, while only a handful of representatives of the environmental community appeared, even in the urban locations. It looked as though they were not as dedicated as they claimed, because few, besides paid representatives, showed up to voice their opinions.

Meanwhile Nye County was planning the confrontation that would throw the federal land management agencies into confusion and bring national attention to the high desert valleys of Nevada. Since the weakest link in federal jurisdiction seemed to be over roads on the public lands. Nye County already had thousands of miles of roads to maintain but the Commissioners decided to add another one

The Battle of Jefferson Canyon

to the maintenance list. Nye County planned to open a road---across proclaimed Federal property.

When the Tonopah Forest Service found out that the county was about to take actions into their own hands, the agency made an effort to split the commission and attempted to get the road opening stopped. The commissioners were sought out by telephone and in person and urged to back down from their position on the matter.

It is immensely difficult to find any body of five individuals who can withstand such an assault by a federal agency. There is almost always a weak link somewhere in the group. But the Nye County Commission never wavered. Commission Chairman, Cameron McRae along with fellow commissioners, Joe Maslach, Red Copas and Dave Hanigan all linked arms with Dick Carver and stood their ground.

There was going to be an unusual Independence Day `celebration in Jefferson Canyon.

THE BATTLE OF JEFFERSON CANYON

This is the reprinted story by Lee Pitts and Don Bowman, which appeared in the *Livestock Market Digest*, July 1994:

Jefferson Canyon is the site of historic Spanish silver mines and like many Nevada boom towns was once the home to thousands of people. Now it is best known for one very important road. But not just any road. This thoroughfare was first established as a toll road between the mining camps of Belmont and Jefferson in the 1870's according to Jeanne Howerton. Jeanne knows a thing or two about the road because her great uncle maintained and operated the toll road. After the silver was extracted the toll booth was abandoned and the unrestrained public use of the road began.

Enter Dick Carver and his fellow Nye County Commissioners who contend that the Forest Service never owned the road in the first place because they never bought it from the Nevada legislature. After all, that is one of the constitutional requirements for the federal ownership of property. Carver made requests of the Forest Service to prove that they did, in fact, own the road but the Forest Service could not furnish the asked for documents. That was when Carver made plans for a big Fourth of July celebration to take back the road and fix it for the use of county residents. They'd throw a little tea over the side of the canyon just to make sure the symbolism was not lost on anybody.

need to do is strengthen it. As an elected official I have a duty to protect your rights." Then he climbed up into the seat of a Nye County bulldozer, put the machine into gear and pulled back the throttle, sending a puff of black smoke above the crowd. For those in attendance it was better than a fireworks display.

Dave Young held the warning sign over his head in the hot sun for about an hour as Carver and the county bulldozer backed him through the pinion trees and rocks of Jefferson Canyon. The Nye County Deputy Sheriff stood on the side and watched as the two played out their hands. Tired and sweaty, Young finally rolled up his sign and Carver proceeded with his work. Young was overheard to comment, "I knew Carver could outlast me because he had a full tank of fuel."

Carver later warned Young that standing directly in front of a bulldozer is not a good place to be. "Don't step in front of me, next time, stand to the side and hold your sign. It's not smart to stand in front of a bulldozer," Carver said.

When Carver finally climbed off the dozer, he addressed the crowd once again, thanking them for coming. As a show of solidarity almost every spectator, man, woman, and child, pitched in by throwing rocks off the road. Carver told the crowd he was confident that the county would prevail.

But Dick Carver was not waiting for any further study. On July 6, just two days after the battle in Jefferson Canyon, Richard Carver walked into the Nye County Sheriff's Office and swore out a criminal complaint against the District Ranger and the Special Investigator. The total complaint was some fifty pages of exhibits and charged them with interfering with a public official. If the District Attorney finds enough fact in the complaint formal charges will be brought and if convicted the men would lose their jobs.

Even more than fireworks or a Fourth of July parade this small skirmish at Jefferson Canyon was a sure sign that the spirit of independence on which this country was founded is alive and well.

The story ended just like Carver hoped it would. No one got hurt and the county still had it's old bulldozer.

The article in the Livestock Digest was not the only paper to carry a story. The *Gateway Gazette* also featured the road opening by Dave Downing, the only other journalist on the scene that day and the Elko Daily Free Press carried a front page article with my story and Dave's pictures. That day turned out to be the biggest photo opportunity in the country and my camera produced two rolls of film that were completely **BLACK!**

The Battle of Jefferson Canyon

I compared notes with Dave Downing in April of 1996. Dave said he was amazed that all the major media had their heads stuck in the sand on that July day in 1994. Dave and I both felt we were chronicling a historic event and felt the Jefferson Canyon skirmish was the story of the year. Even though we both had numerous reprint requests, it was almost a year later the incident became the focus of national attention.

A half mile of road in a heretofore obscure canyon was what the whole fight was about.

HIT THE ROAD, SMOKEY
. . . . .   More Roads Opened by Nye County

Nye County had found a niche in the federal fortress. County domination over roads and access to the public lands seemed to be a real possibility. There was argument as to the ability of the federal agents to arbitrarily close off areas.

During the following months, when anyone who telephoned Carver or supporter Esmerelda County Commissioner Wade Barton, and asked how they were, would hear a laugh and the reply , "Well, we're not in jail, yet."

In the fall of 1994, the road issue came up again in the northern end of Nye County, Nevada. Nye County Commissioners, Richard Carver and Joe Maslach, along with public works director, Bob Wickendon drove to San Juan Canyon in the Reese River Valley. They were met by Lander County Commissioner, Ray Williams, Lander's road superintendent, Jerry Utter and Jim Champie, a local rancher who has deeded land on the road. Dayle Flanigan, the supervisor for the Austin District of the USFS, was waiting for the group at the Forest Service Camp.

Just above the Camp were three large holes in the road, dug by the Forest Service two years before, to prevent vehicles from continuing up the canyon. Carver told Flanigan, "This is ridiculous. If the county did something like this, OSHA would eat us alive." The first hole could be driven into very easily if a driver was not paying attention or

The Battle of Jefferson Canyon

if the light was poor or during a snow storm. It was clearly a public hazard according to the commissioners.

Farther up the Canyon, Dayle Flanigan pointed out where the USFS was going to build a turnaround (about a mile and a half short of where the road at one time entered a patented mining claim). When asked about a date for completion, Flanigan estimated some time in 1995.

Carver wanted to look at options to improve the road on up the canyon and the contingent set off for an overview. Commissioner Maslach insisted that they do the job right if they were going to do it at all. Both Ray Williams and Jim Champie said the road should be put up on a bench that goes along the creek for about a mile, and the Nye County officials agreed.

Ranger Flanigan said that they had to go through the planning process with the Forest Service and get permission. Carver said, "The commissioners have this road on the agenda for Tuesday, Dayle." The ranger repeated his statement. Carver replied with, "I told you we are going to discuss this road at the Tuesday meeting. If you want input, be there." Flanigan said he had other important matters to attend to and that he could not make the meeting.

It was at this time that Carver asked Flanigan his three questions regarding ownership, jurisdiction and delegated authority. Called the Carver Recipe, the three questions were instilled into Dick's mind by Ed Presley, who claimed jurisdiction should be established, before anything else is discussed:

The CARVER RECIPE for RELIEF

There are only three main ingredients, and yet they would send the federal employees away seething, every time, on public land issues.

Carver would ask for the federal officials to produce the following:

1. The DOCUMENTATION showing they own the land in question.

2. The DOCUMENTATION showing they have constitutional   jurisdiction over the land.

3. The DOCUMENTATION proving the Federal employee has   proper delegated authority.

Dick kept telling people to not take the federal employees word for anything. These questions should be asked every time. Commissioner Eve Culverwell, of Lincoln County, Nevada, asks to see the deed for the land, because after all, the feds can produce a deed for military installations and needful buildings.

The feds would usually come back with the reply that they have the right to manage federal property. There is no

argument for that statement. Of course they can. But Carver says, "Let's make sure that it is federal property involved in the issue."
Every citizen and especially every county commissioner should have this recipe committed to memory, according to Carver.

Flanigan recited the National Environment Protection Act rules and Federal property statements from some papers he was carrying. Carver told Dayle that his answer would have worked in the past, but, "all this land changed status as of November 5, 1993." When Flanigan questioned him about the significance of that date, Carver said, "That is when I mailed my letter (proclaiming state ownership) to the Secretary of the Interior and the Secretary of Agriculture."

Dayle's face grew a puzzled expression, while Jim Champie and Ray Williams burst out laughing. Maybe the change in status of the lands was a little far reaching, but Nye County had definitely changed the status of the roads.

The group then moved to adjacent Cottonwood Canyon to look at the road closure there. Flanigan said that the stream in the canyon was designated as a habitat to the threatened Lahontan Cutthroat Trout. Joe Maslach said that it must be the 184th stream designated as such in Nye County and that he did not think the County had been notified on the matter.

Upon arriving at the closure point just above Jim Champie's land in Cottonwood Canyon, Carver again took Flanigan to task, "Here we have a rancher, Jim Champie, who has been allowing the public access across his land and the Forest Service is trying to DENY the people access to the public land. This is downright ridiculous."

Carver said that since the roads were so close to the Lander County border, he might ask for assistance from his neighboring county. Lander County had endorsed the action and enacted a resolution of support for opening the road.

The Nye County Commission voted to open the roads in San Juan and Cottonwood Canyons in Northern Nye County on October 15, 1994. The Commission also approved an interlocal agreement and sent it to Lander county for ratification by that county.

The Commission also approved the request by a mining company to repair a road into its claims, on the east side of the same mountain range. The US Forest Service had required a $300,000 bond for the mining company to do the work previously, but the Commission said that since the road is a county road by their statutes, they could approve the work.

Dayle Flanigan of the Austin Ranger District was on hand and protested that the roads came under RS 2477 designation. (Roads in place before 1976 when the National Environmental Protection Act was put into law were said to be RS 2477 roads. Roads after that date were at risk of being closed by the government. There had been a push by the BLM and USFS to force the counties to map any roads of this nature, without providing funding to do so, by the way.)

The Commission informed him that the roads were not roads of that designation, but county roads and that even if they had been RS 2477 roads, the 9th circuit Court of Appeals in response to an Alaska case had ruled within the last year that access could not be denied or restricted. In fact the Ninth Circuit ruled that:

* An RS 2477 is a right-of-way to travel from one point to another and is not limited to a precise route.

* Continuous use is not a requirement.

* The condition of the highway, whether paved, wagon-worthy or simply a footpath, is irrelevant if the claimant can show the right-of -way was used.

* The manner of travel(by foot, beast or vehicle) is legally irrelevant to the RS 2477 determination. What matters is that the right-of-way was used for travel between two definite points.

After the ruling, BLM and USFS employees started interpreting the decision as being in effect only over snow-covered ground in Alaska, even though the ruling did not talk about snow cover. They were now saying the decision had no bearing on lands outside Alaska and were continuing with their previous policy. They evidently believed Nevada roads did not lie within the 9th Circuit because they were going to ignore the ruling.

Not all federal employees believed in this interpretation, and one gave Dick Carver copies of the Congressional Act of February 25, 1885, which said no one, by unlawful means, can obstruct passage across the public lands. In essence, this law gives carte blanche passage across the land. The employee said this act was subsequent to the 1872 mining law, which dealt with RS 2477 and only addressed, *"construction of roads, over lands NOT reserved for public use."* RS 2477 was being misread and misapplied by the BLM, USFS, and many attorneys, who are always complaining about people not reading all of a document, including the commas.

So there were a few federal employees that believed people should have all the available information. There were some bureaucrats with a conscience and some backbone who were helping Nye County!

This meeting led to yet another skirmish. The resistance army and the battlefield was about to increase in size.

The Battle of Jefferson Canyon

TWO COUNTIES OPEN ROAD

The line between Lander County and Nye County, Nevada was obliterated on October 15, 1994 first by about 6 inches of softly falling snow and then by an interlocal agreement between the two counties for just one purpose: The two commissions had voted to undertake a project in concert with one another, specifically to open the road the Forest Service had closed in San Juan Canyon on the northern edge of Nye County. This road had been closed by the USFS some two years before for the purpose, the Forest Service said, of wildlife protection.

On October 13, USFS Ranger Dayle Flanigan sent a letter to the commissions stating that the agency's research team had found no evidence that road rights had been perfected. It further stated that there were numerous archeological and historic artifacts in the vicinity of the roads, as well as sensitive riparian vegetation and habitat.

Jim Champie, whose cattle graze in the canyon, said the roads had been in use since the 1700's and that silver had been transported out of the patented mining claim in the fifties. (The roads are shown on some maps.)

The Flanigan letter closed by saying, "Any activity to maintain, construct, reconstruct, or open these roads to travel without authorization from the Forest Service will be subject to criminal penalties under 16 USC 551 and 36 CFR 26 (federal laws and rules) for failure to obtain authorization and violation of the closure order. Furthermore, the responsible parties will be held accountable for any damages to resources from constructing, or from travel that occurs as a consequence of opening the road."

On the morning of the opening, vehicles were strung out along the snow packed Reese River road for almost a half mile as the people gathered for the drive into San Juan Canyon. Without Lander County's assistance, the day would have been a flop because the snowstorm had become so fierce that the lowboy truck hauling the Nye County bulldozer could not negotiate the Austin Summit and had to turn back. Because of the absence of Nye County equipment, Lander Commissioner Ray Williams said, "We are already furnishing a backhoe and a dump truck so I guess we will have to throw in the loader that is just down the road a ways." One of the road department employees was dispatched to drive the machine into the canyon.

Nye County Commissioner Richard Carver and Lander County Commissioner Ray Williams stood on a Lander County loader to address the crowd, estimated at 150 people from the local area and surrounding counties. Surprisingly, many of the candidates for office showed up to brave the wind-driven snow and put up with cold feet in this beautiful mountain canyon just to watch what would ordinarily be ordinary county work.

The evening of October 14, 1995, just preceding the road opening in San Juan Canyon, was candidates night in Austin,

The Battle of Jefferson Canyon

Nevada. Surprisingly, the main issue was whether the candidates supported the takeover of public lands by the county governments. Both men in the sheriff's races were asked if they would allow the Bureau of Land Management and the Forest Service to have arrest authority. Frank Hobbs said, "Hell no, let them go play their games somewhere else." His opponent agreed.

Rachael Nicholson who was running for the District Attorney's job said there were other ways to get what the counties wanted and that cooperation and understanding within the agencies and the county was useful. However, when Patty Cafferata stepped up she made no bones, "If you want to take on the federal government, I'm here to help you." Nicholson lost, but went to work as a Nye County Deputy District Attorney.

In the same election, Lander County had presented a ballot question asking if the county should continue to assert control over the public lands and the question was approved by 75% of the people.

It was politically sound to support the rebels in Nye and Lander County in 1994. To show up at the San Juan road opening would leave no doubt where the candidates stood on the matter.

Carver said, "We are here to open this road for the safety and welfare of the citizens. This road was closed in a dangerous manner by digging huge holes. Someone could have come down through here on a four wheeler and fallen in one of these and drowned in the water filling the hole. Also I wanted to ask the Forest Service one more time to prove they own the land, have constitutional jurisdiction and proper delegated authority but I don't see Dayle (USFS supervisor), so I guess I can't."

Ray Williams, who later ran the backhoe for a while, said that Lander County was proud to be part of the effort. He also stated that there was deeded ground higher in the canyon and that this road would renew the access to that land. "This also opens a larger part of the mountain for better fire protection," he added.

Carver closed with, "We have two Nye County Deputy Sheriffs, Ray East and Bill Winters here to keep the peace. They are here to arrest anyone who interferes in the opening of this road. Let's get to work."

The district ranger had been at the site while people were arriving but was seen only once during the actual work. The Forest Service did not bring in an armed special investigator as they had in Jefferson Canyon in July. Some people said that maybe they did not have the jurisdiction and had given up. Many were mystified by the lack of response of the USFS. Unlike the confrontation in Jefferson Canyon, there was no personal notification to stop. The federal agencies may have gotten smarter, because one way to avoid doing the wrong thing is to do nothing.

The Battle of Jefferson Canyon

Dick Carver packed rock in the Lander loader to fill the water-saturated hole as Jerry Utter, Lander County Road Supervisor, finished up the last of the three holes with the backhoe. Progress was slow because the snow made for poor traction and the operators had to pay constant attention to avoid injuring bystanders.

Local folks were joined by sympathetic supporters from around the west. Ed Presley, of CARES (County Alliance to Restore the Environment and the Economy) had flown in to inform the people that his alliance and the Individual Rights Foundation out of Los Angeles would be defending the counties or any individual that needed help in this issue, free of charge.

Gracious people from Humboldt County, Nevada provided hamburgers, hot dogs, and chorizo cooked on a smoking fire surrounded by elated Nevadans. Food and yarns were shared indiscriminately throughout the afternoon.

When Dick Carver climbed down off the loader, he thanked the people again for coming and voiced his appreciation to Lander County. He then said, "I think we should send the Forest Service a bill for fixing what they tore up. "

Nye County was going to become famous for its road department.

CATRON COUNTY, AN ECONOMY SHIPWRECKED

A role model for Nye and other counties began its quest for county control some years before. In fact, they are blamed to this day by many federal agencies for starting the whole conflagration.

Even before Carver started down the road to attempt government reform, another county had given the first push against the chest of the federal government.

Catron County had its whole economy gut shot by the federal land management agencies. The biggest producers of jobs in the county were timber and mining, while the only other major industry was ranching. Federal agency action by the U.S. Forest Service had completely stopped timber harvest, shut down the mine, and seriously crippled grazing.

A county of only 3000 people, with a disgruntled board of commissioners and a stand-up County Attorney, decided it was time for someone make a move. Catron County, New Mexico was the first entity to take any major county action, which later incited like moves by many more counties across the West.

Dick Manning, a New Mexico rancher, who was having serious problems with the federal agencies, managed to get the ear of a good attorney who worked on issues such as those facing the people of Catron County. This lawyer whose interest he piqued was a young Wyoming woman,

The Battle of Jefferson Canyon

Karen Budd.   Dick put into motion a tenacious, smart lawyer who was going to help break new ground.

Karen Budd was later hailed as one of the figures who would have a large part in shaping the new West. She was raised on a ranch and had on the ground, first hand knowledge of the livestock industry. Karen's father, Dan Budd, who was a rancher and a former Wyoming legislator, carried a copy of the Constitution around in his shirt pocket while performing his duties as a state elected official. Karen said that the carrying of the document was not just for show, because he would pull it out and refer it many times while working on laws. Karen's father was very conscious of people's rights and always considered them when taking any actions. Karen continued the legacy by fighting for the rights of the rural counties of the West.

Karen   teamed up with the Catron County Attorney, James Catron, and the two began pouring over regulations. They discovered that there were a LOT of rules requiring federal agencies to seek the counsel of the local governments when implementing actions. They found that local custom and culture were supposed to be addressed when Environmental Impact Studies were done. The federal agencies had been ignoring the rules, in effect working much like a monarchy which only answers to a king. The two attorneys drafted the first ordinances requiring the federal government to listen to a county voice.

Budd and James Catron put together a magnificent plan, with the help of Ron White, Carl Hess, Alex Thal, and Howard Hutchinson.

Howard, who compiled a lot of the research, was a former member of Earth First, a radical environmental group, which had developed a falsely-founded hatred for ranching, logging and mining. Howard said that when he first became a member of the group in 1980, Earth First believed in the concept of protection at the local level. They believed that by living in and making themselves a part of the community, they could exert the pressures necessary for protection of the environment.

Howard was in for a huge awakening. He said, "As I became a part of the community, I realized that my neighbors shared the same values that I shared." Howard's neighbors all wanted clean water, a healthy forest, clean air and abundant game. Moreover, by living with and in their own geography, they knew most of what was wrong and what was needed to fix it. They also wanted the ecology maintained for their children. This didn't sound like a bunch of people who were out to rape the land, as his fellow members believed.

Howard said that as Earth First's agenda became more directed toward private property and people, he began to have misgivings about the group's way of doing business. When monkey-wrenching or eco-terrorism (trashing people's property and killing livestock) came into being, Howard said it was time to call it quits. Instead of busting up ranchers' and miners' improvements, he started to work,

The Battle of Jefferson Canyon

helping to rectify his county with good science and positive actions. Later, Howard was picked to be coordinator for the Arizona/New Mexico Coalition of Counties and was a lobbyist in Sante Fe for an agriculture group. Howard had defected and was working on the other side helping to formulate a county plan.

The plan was later named the Catron County Plan, which became known and admired, throughout the West. The plan, using the federal rules which were already in place, required the federal agencies to consult with the county on issue affecting the local custom, culture, and economy. The concept became a model for many other local governments whose officials were tired of the feds ramming one decision after another down their throats and into a belly already soured by an overdose of bureaucracy. The County Plan looked to be the savior of the depressed counties. Hell, the federal agencies HAD to abide by their own rules, didn't they? Committees were established and Memorandums of Understanding (MOU's) were drafted, agreed upon, and signed between the county, and the USFS and the BLM. The plan looked to be a winner.

Livestock Market Digest editor, Lee Pitts, wrote a story about the plan. He said he had never written anything that created so much excitement. Catron County office phones were ringing off the hook. This obscure little county became the hope of thousands of rural people across the country. Catron County had kindled a fire of revolt without guns.

The National Federal Lands Conference pitched in to help disseminate information. The NFLC was and is devoted to maintaining and dispersing data for education and assistance of the rural economies.

Two years later an environmental group called the Gila Watch filed suit against Catron County, claiming the new ordinances caused them harm, and asked the ordinances be struck down. The court found the group could not prove harm and let the ordinances stand. A similar case was upheld by the Ninth Circuit Court in early 1996.

Three years after the plan was adopted, the federal agencies, in spite of signing the MOU's, were reneging on their contracts with the county, and ignoring the agreements and continued to make decisions without allowing the county any input. But now, the county had an army of support, springing up across the country as one county after another legislates some form or another of home rule ordinances or resolutions. Although Nye County received more publicity, Catron County was the first to take a stand.

While Nye County and Catron County were wrestling with the bureaucrats, another Nevada County was addressing the economics of local management of the public lands. This county had the information every taxpayer should know. Eureka County was tackling the core issues; economic cost, practical management, and sustainability.

The Battle of Jefferson Canyon

WE CAN DO IT BETTER

In 1995, Eureka County, Nevada funded a study which showed the feasibility of county management of the public lands. The study, by Resource Concepts of Carson City, Nevada, showed that neighboring states derived a profit from the management of their state lands.

Eureka County paid some $68,000 for, the study, which looked at several state's revenues and was conducted to address the apprehensions concerning the viability of county management.

The Bureau of Land Management in Nevada showed a 1994 budget of 42.5 million dollars. Officials said another 10.5 million was spent for fire suppression and 5 million more for fire related expenditures. The state received 18.4 million in PILT (Payment in lieu of taxes, on federal lands) funds and other shared revenue from the feds, according to the budget department. This amounts to 79.2 million dollars out of the federal coffers. The agency derived some 21.2 million dollars in revenue that year. If this is true, the burden on the American taxpayer for Nevada BLM management was over 50 million dollars per year in 1994.

Arizona BLM employees said their budget was 27.2 million dollars in 1994, not counting money spent for fire control. This amounts to about $1.90 per acre for the 14.2

million acres of BLM managed lands in Arizona. When the Arizona BLM was questioned about funds spent on fires, they said that information was not available, because fire expenditures came from a fund that all the agencies tapped for fire control.

Nevada's sister state, Arizona, derived a net profit of 40 to 50 million dollars per year from their management program. Gene Gustin, Elko County Public Lands Advisory Commission Chairman, said these figures show the possibility of a 100 million dollar turn around for Nevada, by taking a 50 million dollar plus loss and turning it into a profit.

Arizona's Governor, Fyfe Symington, had previously called the federal control of the lands bizarre, costly, and poorly managed to boot. Symington said, "With the State of Arizona managing its own public lands, the state could save the American Taxpayer 50 million dollars per year."

Bob Yount, the director of the grazing program for Arizona said the State of Arizona was charging $1.35 per AUM (animal unit month) for grazing in 1995. There are 8.4 million acres of state lands under the management of 8 people for grazing. Yount said, "Our purpose is to make money, not burden the taxpayers with costs. By state law, we do not have a requirement to go through an Environmental Impact Statement on every issue. However, we do solicit comments from the same kinds of people you would use for an EIS, such as the Fish and Game, water resources, etc."

The Battle of Jefferson Canyon

The agency also does internal review on its actions and they have an environmental trespass section for enforcement of violations.

In January of 1996, Arizona Assemblyman, Joe Hart said that he had documentation from the federal government showing that 25.7 billion dollars were taken in nationally from oil, gas and coal revenues and the BLM was running a 300 million dollar a year deficit. He said that Arizona proves yearly that land can be managed at a profit.

At that time, former director of the Bureau of Land Managment, Sy Jamison concurred with Hart and added that the BLM and USFS probably had a 500 million dollar a year loss between them.

No wonder the bureaucrats were happy about the radical environmental plans, because with plans like those, their jobs were getting bigger and better. Land management, one of the largest industries in the nation, had become a top-heavy, inefficient organization that would have toppled long ago if it had been a private enterprise. The American taxpayer, as usual, was footing the bills for another government program that came far from giving them their money's worth. Even worse, while the feds were raping the taxpayers, they were creating havoc in the rural economies.

Eureka County, Nevada was not just whining and waiting. The county had done the one thing that should have been done by the states and the federal government a long time ago. Someone should have taken a hard look at what was taking place in the federal management of public lands, then worked toward solving the problems. After funding one study, the county followed up with another. Even better, the county hired a resource manager, whose first job was to study actual management applications of the agencies.

Eureka County hired a resource manager whose commission was to research the methods of range assessment and management of the federal agencies and to begin planning for local management. Their idea was we can do it better. Now, let's prove it.

John Balliette, Eureka County Resource Manager, has a bachelor's degree in animal science and range science, with a doctorate in range science from the University of Texas. John worked for the BLM for one year and called it "The most miserable year of my life." He said that it was criminal the way bureau wasted so much money. He contended the agency stultified personal initiative so badly that they made it impossible for anyone with diverse ideas and common sense to do a job.

In the early 1980's, Eureka County had 40,000 head of cattle on the tax rolls plus 9000 head of sheep. Now there were roughly 11,000 head of cattle and 3000 head of sheep in the county.

The Battle of Jefferson Canyon

Market factors and changes in range condition were part of the reason for the reduction, but John says he believes that most of the cuts were due to government intervention.

Balliette started doing studies, using the BLM's own methodology. One case study involved a ranch with an original adjudication of forage that the BLM was trying to cut in half. The agency was basing the cuts on utilization data they had compiled from two to four years earlier. John assessed the BLM's methodology in December of 1995 on a tract of 100,000 acres. He found that 86,000 acres had not been used by the BLM to determine carrying capacity, truly an unfair way to assess rangeland.

In this and many other cases, the agents would find what they considered to be the poorest range conditions, even if they were on only a small portion of range, and portray it as being the condition of the whole allotment. In the example above only 14,000 acres (or 14% of the allotment) were used in the survey performed by the BLM. The BLM did not perform surveys in 1994 or 1995, which were both good years for range forage production.

John collected utilization for 1995 and could document that the vast majority of the allotment, close to 69 percent, received slight or light usage.

John made a recalculation of carrying capacity of the range and came up with an amount greater than the amount of the original grazing adjudication of the ranch.

Because of BLM actions like these, financing sources which had traditionally been strong backers of western ranchers were now saying that they would not fund any more acquisitions of ranches with public land dependency.

A rancher who was in trouble in 1995 and had to sell was now in even more trouble financially because his ranch was devalued first by the slumping cattle market, then by agency cuts.

The BLM officials claimed they had to let all interested parties, most of whom were members of the Sierra Club, Audubon Society, etc., have input on each proposed action. Most of these people lived 200 miles or more away. John Balliette thought that the most interested parties should be the people of the county where the actions were implemented. Shortly, there were requests for notification of BLM proposals on store counters, in banking establishments, and in the hands of some ranch wives, who were headed to get signatures. The resulting flood of mail to the federal offices left the bureaucrats with little time for anything but making copies and licking stamps. It was joked that the BLM was running out of spit.

Little Eureka County was causing the Battle Mountain BLM District to have a regulation gas pain that they never anticipated. They were beginning to find that the rules that

The Battle of Jefferson Canyon

had been made and stuffed down the rancher's throats were choking the very system that made them.

While they were working on the matter, the county also organized a structure for management of the public lands and were ready to take over when the time came.

Eureka County's neighbor, Elko County staged a rebellion of its own.

ELKO COUNTY WATERS DOWN USFS

Elko County, Nevada rancher, Don Duval had developed a spring on the public lands, turning a trickle of water into useful watering hole for his livestock and wildlife that used the water.

The U. S. Forest Service wanted Duval to remove the improvements he had made and Don refused. The agency took the matter to court and obtained a court order requiring the removal of the fence protecting the spring and the pipeline feeding the watering trough. Don, to avoid being held in contempt of court, complied, taking out the improvements in the fall of 1994.

Shortly after Duval finished taking out the improvements, 500 people from Elko County calling themselves the Kelly Spring Protective Association, organized by local attorney Grant Gerber, began moving to *reinstall* the spring box and a protective fence around the projec!. Grant Gerber said that the State of Nevada recognized Duval's right to the spring and that the USFS was trying to circumvent Nevada water law. The Elko reclamation party formed up one morning, loaded up fencing supplies and pipe, drove out to the site, and replaced everything Duval had removed, but with *better* construction. Each steel post was inscribed with the name of one of the rebuilders. *The Elko Daily Free Press* called the action, "The Ruby Valley Tea Party."

The Forest Service let the new improvements stand, evidently unwilling to oppose such a huge demonstration of public opinion.

The Battle of Jefferson Canyon

The Elko County Commission decided to take an active role in the Kelly Spring contoversey and filed a lawsuit asking the court affirm individual's rights to maintain their water transportation rights of way under state law and without obtaining permits from a federal agency even though the easement may be across public land. The case was dismissed by the judge who said the county did not have standing in the matter.

During the spring of 1995, an under secretary in the Department of Agriculture, Jim Lyons, told a Senate hearing that he was fearful for his employee's safety in Nevada and particularly in Elko County. The USFS local office and the state office was asked repeatedly if there were any documented threats to their employees. Local offices denied there had been any threats and no documents were produced. This lie about federal employees being threatened was repeated several times by Washington bureaucrats, but was never substantiated or justified.

When Lyons asked Attorney General Janet Reno to launch an expedited investigation of Nevadans, Dan Steninger, editor of the *Elko Daily Free Press* wrote this blistering editorial about the idea:

WHAT'S THE PLAN, JANET
SHOOT US OR BURN US OUT?

"The last time the Department of Justice expedited an investigation and took urgent action, scores of men women and children were either shot or burned to death earning Reno the title of the Butcher of Waco. The time before that, the feds snuffed the son and wife of Randy Weaver up in Idaho.

That's what we call hostility.

Yet it is the federal agents who now claim they fear for their safety. We haven't heard of any feds up here getting threatened and, interestingly enough, neither has the county sheriff or the Federal Bureau of Investigation. We'd say the chances of someone taking a poke at a federal agent are a lot less than the chances of Dick Carver being taken out by a federal sniper."

Dan summed up by saying, "If Janet Reno thinks a federal show of force will quash the states' rights movement, we'd point out it was easier to burn a building full of families than it will be to impose martial law on the state of Nevada."

Dan not only took the feds to task but state and local officials as well if it was warranted. No one was immune from Steniger's verbal darts.

Elko County residents garnered enough signatures on a petition in the fall of 1995 to cause the impanelment of a grand jury to investigate the suspected collusion between federal agents and environmentalists and to investigate the

The Battle of Jefferson Canyon

alleged threats to federal employees. Testimony began in early 1996 and would put the federal agencies on the spot to produce documents of the threats, which by now they claimed they had, but would not release for security reasons. Then the court acquiesced to the federal agencies who said they could not let their employees testify because of security reasons. The court topped off by sealing the records from the public.

The Elko County District Attorney brought terrific pressure to bear on the court, saying it was wrong to let the federal government escape scrutiny on such an important matter. *Free Press* editor Dan Steninger took the matter to the Nevada State Supreme Court saying it was wrong to keep the records from the press.

The judge caved in to the immense political pressure brought to bear and ordered the federal employees to testifiy.

The federal agencies were expected to appeal in federal court. As of the date of publishing the facts were not yet available.

The next remarkable skirmish between the counties and the feds took place a lot farther south in Babbitt's home state.

GRAHAM COUNTY, ARIZONA
ROAD AND GUN CLUB

If you had pulled into Safford, Arizona anytime in 1995 and asked for directions to the sheriff's office, some smiling resident would likely have said, "Are you looking for Sheriff Mack? " then obligingly give directions. Richie Mack is looked up to by most of the young people and the business community. Mack became famous for taking the Brady Gun Bill to district court and getting the law ruled as unconstitutional. The ruling was struck down by the Court of Appeals on the grounds that the law did not impose a burden on the states. As of this writing, the case is being appealed to the Supreme Court.

Sheriff Mack said he knew the Brady Bill would violate both U.S. and Arizona Constitutions, which he was sworn to uphold. The right to bear arms should not be impaired and Mack felt that the gun law would not help stem criminal acts, but only impede law-abiding citizens.

Mack is anything but a redneck law officer. This tall, slim sheriff looks like he just stepped off a white horse and leaves no doubt about his beliefs. He is a calm, religious, and conscientious individual, who has gone to great lengths to ensure what he believes to be the basic freedoms of America. He has been featured on television news and articles nationwide and always presents his views very well. Sheriff Mack and Tim Walters have written an eye opening book, *From My Cold Dead Fingers*, which tells about gun control, the Constitution, crime and state sovereignty.

The Battle of Jefferson Canyon

Graham County, Arizona was home to two environmental issues that defied common sense: The blocking of the building of the Mount Graham International Observatory and the bridge across the Gila river.

Tim Walter's next books, *Surviving the Second Civil War* and *The Endangered American Dream*, document the whole story of Mount Graham and other strange and unfathomable happenings of the time. The following facts are from Tim's books:

Mount Graham is a forested peak surrounded by desert and known to be situated in some of the clearest air on the planet. The observatory occupies less than 15 acres of a 300 square mile mountain island, surrounded by desert. Congress designated 3500 acres of the mountain as a potential astrophysical research study area in 1984. Since then, the University of Arizona has run into a series of the most mind-boggling, ridiculous, roadblocks imaginable in its effort to build a series of observatories. Construction of the first telescope began in 1989 and was to eventually include two additional scopes. That summer the Sierra Club Legal Defense Fund filed a lawsuit against the U.S. Forest Service and the U.S. Fish and Wildlife. The suit claimed that the construction of an observatory would disrupt the red squirrel habitat and lead to extinction of the subspecies. Federal regulations were being used to stop a state university project.

Three years of court battles, which sporadically held up progress on the site, ended with the district court and the appeals court throwing out the claims. In the spring of 1994 two telescopes were finally in use on the mountain. Subsequent radical suits have forced the University of Arizona to abandon its expansion plan for the site, regardless of the fact that the expansion would not double the amount of land needed. Even though wildlife was shown to be increasing and the proposed development would disturb little of the existing forest, some groups continued to object and were constantly grabbing for any foothold they could use against the school.

The Gila River crossing is the story of a quick solution to ridiculous requirements. Sheriff Mack was not the only person in Graham County with guts enough to make a stand for whatever he thinks is right. The county board of supervisors have also had their day on the battlefield, and like in Nye County, Nevada, just did what they thought was right.

The three man board applied to the Army Corps of Engineers for a permit to replace a damaged bridge over the Gila River, washed out in 1993. The bridge and its approaches had been a part of the Graham County road system for years. It sounds simple and should have been an easy thing to acquire, but that was not the case. The Corps held up permits on advice of the U.S. Fish and Wildlife Service, who was concerned about an endangered razorback suckerfish, which had been unsuccessfully *planted* there by the Arizona Game and Fish! USFWS Supervisor Sam

The Battle of Jefferson Canyon

Spiller decided that the purpose and need statement for the bridge was inadequate. The bridge, if constructed would force the river on a course that would stop the current drastic erosion of the farmland along the river, something Spiller was in favor of letting continue. Protection of species was the only mission the USFWS was interested in or willing to hear about.

Graham County Supervisor, Terry Bingham asked Sam Spiller, "When do we consider people in this?"

To which Spiller replied, "We don't."

The Gila River is a half mile wide gravel bed with a small stream coursing through it for most of the year. The river serves a huge drainage area that reaches far into New Mexico and every couple of years turns into a massive destructive force as large as the Colorado River during a 100 year flood. The gravel bottom is disturbed radically during a flood stage. Huge runoffs of water tear out banks, deposit huge amounts of debris and earth in different places and drastically change plant and animal communities that have built up between floods. Sometimes nothing is left but a bare bottom with banks denuded and former fish and wildlife habitat wiped out. The results would be the same as someone constructing a freeway right in the river course from one side of the state to the other. No amount of bulldozing on one small stretch can come close to nature's almost annual event. However, this made no difference to the Corps or the USFWS.

The huge wide, flat bottom can make bridge building an expensive proposition, so the supervisors decided a low water crossing on the river bottom was needed, to temporarily take the traffic, while the feds got their act in order. The supervisors asked for permission to make the crossing and were denied again! County Manager Joe Carter wrote to President Clinton, asking for bureaucratic relief. Governor Symington appealed to Newt Gingrich and county officials pleaded with congressmen, to no avail. The USFWS was a deaf, uncaring roadblock on the Gila River bridge.

The washed out section of road made the school bus ride for a load of children lengthen from 2 miles to 26 miles, one way. Cotton farmers had to drive heavy machinery the same distance.

The supervisors decided they were going to build the crossing without permission, even though they were threatened by the Corps of Engineers. The Corps notified the county that each of the supervisors could face fines exceeding $50,000 and imprisonment up to three years if a temporary crossing were installed without the necessary permits.

The supervisors decided that it was within their jurisdiction to maintain the health and safety of their community and authorized the work. A few steel culverts were placed in the stream bed and a road was graded across the expanse of dry river bed. The school bus and the residents again made use of the road they had been traveling for years, thanks to their leaders, who would not be buffaloed by the bureaucrats.

The federal government did not challenge the county's actions, which the county claimed were within their constitutional powers. Another county in the West has said, "This is our county and we are going to take care of our people!"

This county does take care of its people. When Tim Walters suffered a heart attack, ending up with huge medical bills and no insurance, the residents held benefit functions, lifting a large part of the financial burden from Tim's shoulders. Tim figured he would repay the debt by running for supervisor in 1996. If elected, Tim promised he would continue to strive to protect his county's jurisdiction and its people.

THE 94 ELECTION

While Graham County was wrestling with the federal agencies, Nevada politicians were being forced to further address the public lands issue.

Elko County Lands Board Chairman, Gene Gustin happily reported in July of 1994 that the upcoming election was beginning to make the Elko County Commissioners more aware of the importance of the public land issues. The public lands debate was beginning to be a focal point of the election in many of the other Nevada rural counties.

The central counties striving for control had developed a name for the movement to acquire local control of the public lands, calling it the *Nevada Plan for Public Land.* Wade Barton of Esmerelda County made up blue and silver banners and bumper stickers. Many car bumpers were adorned with "The Nevada Plan."

The Nevada Alliance for Public Lands staged an information meeting in Winnemucca, Nevada on October 1, to educate people of the district on the hot topic of federal jurisdiction. The gathering ended up being a forum for political candidates who were stumping the state to drum up votes.

Jim Gibbons, who was the GOP candidate for governor of Nevada said, "The Nevada Plan is too important to ignore. I am damn mad about the failure of the Governor and the Attorney General to respond to the counties' request for land for their county needs." (Gibbons is talking about requests made by Nye County and Lander County for land to establish solid waste dumps, land for county buildings, and a recreation area).

"Governor Miller does not understand the Constitution," Gibbons declared, "We the people of Nevada must have control of the public lands." He also said that the legislature needed to be better educated on the powers of government. As an example, he stated that Nevada had 130 years of water right law which was working and that the federal government was trying to make a "can of worms" out of a working concept.

He also said that the original Sagebrush Rebellion (the 1979 movement to reclaim the public lands) was different because it did not address the underlying ownership of the lands. "And," he added, "The Nevada Plan does just that."

With evident confidence, the candidate said, "I will be anxious to sign the deeds for the counties to acquire public land. If I am Governor, and they (the feds) arrest Dick Carver, then they will have to arrest the Governor also." He complimented Carver and the central counties for their efforts to bring to light the proper and constitutional structure of government.

The November election struck an even balance between the Republicans and the Democrats in the Nevada

Legislature. However, the Republicans were taking over the U.S. House of Representatives. The Clinton administration was going to have an indigestible lump for the next four years. Bruce Babbitt would continue to pursue his environmental agenda, but he would periodically get jerked back by the collar by congressmen who were trying to tone down Babbitt's agenda until they could legislate around him. Things were beginning to change.

After the election there was a lull in the battle and it looked as if the federal government was stymied by Nye County's actions.

Suddenly, in the spring of 1995, the next federal assault against Nye County came on orders from United States Attorney General, Janet Reno.

The Battle of Jefferson Canyon

FEDS FILE SUIT AGAINST NYE COUNTY

In the wake of the events at Jefferson Canyon and San Juan Canyons, the Department of Justice filed suit against Nye County March 8, 1995 in Las Vegas Federal Court. The federal government asked for injunctive relief against Nye County's interference with management of federal lands. The Justice Department stated in their suit, "The United States has no adequate remedy at law to prevent Nye County from continued hindrance." The suit said there were no laws to support federal dominance of the public lands, but wanted the judge to let them to continue, unhindered, to manage and police the public lands. The outcome of the case would affect not only resources, but the allocation of the management jobs, to federal, state, or county employees.

Actual definition of federal lands became a major issue in the case, along with the question of which entities had jurisdiction and management. Nye County, supported by a chapter of Nevada Revised Statutes, contended that the public lands had not been federally acquired by legislation pursuant to the constitution. NRS chapter 328 lists each and every parcel of federal land in the state, and the list is not very long, including post offices, military installations, and Hoover Dam.

National media flooded Nye County with requests for interviews and information on the issue. The phones were ringing constantly in every department, mostly with the question, "How can a little county government afford to take this fight on?" CNN television portrayed the county as arid, mostly uninhabited country, giving the impression that both federal and local governments were battling over something of dubious value. It was thought that if the promised support from sympathetic parties came through, Nye County would not have to spend a lot money on legal fees. The Individual Rights Foundation claimed to have unlimited resources and the legal expertise to take on the fight, free of charge.

Many counties were expected to intervene in their own behalf. Eureka County, Nevada filed for intervener status through their DA's office and offered to include some poorer counties who could not afford to take action. Bill Schaeffer and his deputy, Zane Miles, had conducted extensive research into the equal footing doctrine and produced an extensive brief on the subject. Zane Miles said, "We have been working on this for one and a half years and we are well ahead of Janet Reno's troops." The opinion was written in laymen's terms, so as Zane puts it, "Maybe even the people in the Department of Justice can understand it."

The problem was getting the DOJ to read it. Miles and Schaeffer were both mystified that the DOJ was staffed with attorneys who, they said, would not read the cases. Likewise, at the state level, the Nevada Attorney General had been asked by both the governor's office and researcher Dave Haight to deliver an opinion on the issue. She had

The Battle of Jefferson Canyon

written a reply that said, "I would advise you not to harbor any unfounded expectations about the issuance of an opinion." Bill Schaeffer said, "I guess you would say that the AG is verbally seated on the fence."

At first, The Eureka DA, along with a throng of other attorneys, questioned Carver's state ownership theory, "I went looking for affirmation of the federal government's position, hoping to tell the guys, 'let's quit wasting our time.'" Bill admits that the more he delved into the matter, the more evidence he found to dispute the government's claims. "This issue has been sitting in hibernation for 150 years. What are the chances that no District Attorney or an Attorney General would address this and litigate it in that period of time? What makes me think that Zane and I are the only people to take a hard look at this?"

The Nye County Commission held another meeting in Beatty, Nevada on March 21, 1995 and voted unanimously to proceed with the defense of their stand. They also appointed John Howard of the Individual Rights Foundation and Bill Schaeffer as co-counsels to their DA. Schaeffer opted out as co-counsel because he felt he needed a separate stance for Eureka and other counties he might represent.

Some people, who were horrified at the thought of the federal government suing a county, voiced their concerns. Bill Schaeffer said, "We can't afford not to fight. If we lose, where are we? We are right back answering the central government's beck and call, and nothing has changed. If we win, we win land and tax base not only for Nevada and its people, but for the whole West."

Roger Marzula, a Washington Attorney who formerly worked in the Environment and Natural Resources Division of the Department of Justice, was taken on board as co-counsel by John Howard. Roger said, "I am astonished the government filed such a poorly drafted document." He said he expected more from the division, which he formerly headed.

He stated, "The 8O's Sagebrush Rebellion was not nearly as well organized, or as sophisticated as the one that is going on today." He also said that the merits of the case were with the county and that he expected Nye County to win.

Marzulla further said, "The Nye County case is the most important issue to come before the courts in the last 15O years. The Las Vegas court will have to decide, for the first time in history, who owns the public lands." The county's case was backed by Supreme Court decisions which showed that all states, regardless of what their enabling acts proclaim or regardless of what any federal statute establishes, acquire statehood under a Constitution, which grants *equal* treatment with the original thirteen states. Neither federal nor state lawmakers, according to Marzulla, are able to enact anything contrary to the Constitution and lawfully enforce such acts.

The Battle of Jefferson Canyon

The definition of public lands was another bone of contention in the case. Marzula said that even though the Nevada territorial legislature disclaimed right to the public land, an act beyond their power, the Nevada statehood act said the "United States *shall* sell the public lands and give 5 percent of the net proceeds to the state of Nevada." Nothing was said about the United States keeping the land. According to the Washington attorney, public lands are supposed to be sold and the proceeds applied to the debt of the United States.

The third major point in the Individual Rights Foundation's brief relied on the concept of separation of powers. The federal government claimed in its filing that the county had no voice whatsoever over the public lands. The IRF rebuts that concept. "Here, in effect, the United States is trying to impose a monarchy, in which the U.S. runs 93 percent of the county." Marzulla added, "It's inconsistent with our system and it's a violation of separation of powers between federal and state government." He also said he believed all three of those arguments were ironclad constitutional arguments.

When asked about the image of Nye County, portrayed by many as purely confrontational, the attorney said, "The Clinton Administration picked this fight, not us."

The State of Nevada still dragged its heels. Nevada Attorney General, Frankie Sue Del Papa, declined to intervene on Nye County's behalf, according to the *Nevada Sentinel*. The paper further stated that the AG claimed that the new rebels were relying on faulty legal advice based on archaic Supreme Court decisions. In truth, attorneys for the county were using cases as late as 1992 in their research, namely *New York vs. United States.*

New York prevailed in preventing the federal government from forcing a low-level nuclear dump onto the state of New York. How could these cases be considered archaic?

Eureka County District Attorney, William Schaeffer, said that his office was prepared to adhere to the briefing schedule. Schaeffer said, "We have answered every question. The federal government can't do that."

Argument was scheduled to begin July 28, 1995 in the Federal Courtroom of Judge LLoyd George in Las Vegas, Nevada.

The Battle of Jefferson Canyon

THE TRIAL

LAS VEGAS, JULY 28, 1995. People from across the West braved 113 degree temperatures to witness a hearing on who should control the public lands. The courtroom was filled to capacity and the remainder of the crowd occupied the hall and the downstairs lobby. Spectators were mostly public lands users, but there were also some legislators from Arizona and New Mexico. Two people had come from New Hampshire. One family traveled all the way from Texas, which has no public lands, but was resisting federal pressure on other matters. If there was anyone who was not backing Nye County, they did not make themselves known. One man carried a sign, "Oregon supports Nye County."

Judge Lloyd George rapped the court into session, saying, "I am delighted to see all this interest." He also said that they had not anticipated such a huge crowd and apologized for not having enough space to allow everyone to witness the proceedings. He told the audience that better accommodations would be furnished at any future hearings. He stated that two counties who had filed intervenors, but would not be allowed in on that day. The two counties were Eureka and Lander in Nevada.

"I don't know that we need to take a lot of time," the judge said. He stated that he had read the briefs and wanted only testimony that was not included in the briefs.

He gave each side 20 minutes for opening. After introductions, he told the Department of Justice to lead off.

Kathryn Landreth of the Department of Justice introduced her co-counsel and Assistant AG, Peter Coppelman, who stated the case for the federal government. His statement, contrary to the judge's request, repeated the DOJ brief. The government was charging Nye County with illegally bulldozing roads on federal property, filing criminal charges against federal employees and interceding in grazing issues in Nye County. Coppelman said Nye County was mixing and matching court decisions and Constitution clauses for its own benefit. He said that there was an unbroken line of precedent for 150 years of federal control and that it was unthinkable that Nye County wanted to "redraw the map." He said that if the county wanted a voice in issues, it could take advantage of the federal statutes allowing county input.

The Nye County District Attorney, Bob Beckett, next took the podium and said there had been no charges pressed against federal employees. He introduced his special counsels, John Howard and Roger Marzula.

John Howard refuted the suggestion that the federal government would allow local input in the future. Howard said, "County after county has been denied voice in management. Mr. Coppelman evidently does not believe in true equality." Howard reiterated time and again, "*No condition* can be imposed on a new state that was not applied to the original thirteen."

The Battle of Jefferson Canyon

"Furthermore, no condition in an enabling act (statehood act) can defeat the title to the land," Howard told the Judge, who interrupted him several times, asking questions to help clarify points made. Howard told the court that the next three states to achieve statehood after the original thirteen, had not given up public land. Among his remarks were, "Only when the public lands have been disposed of, will the states attain true equality. Where is the sovereignty of the State of Nevada? This case is not about land, it is about the system," He cited several Supreme Court decisions upholding his theory. He and the judge agreed that no such issue had ever been before a court.

Roger Marzula, who is blind, steadily took notes on a braille printer as involved parties spoke on the issue. He picked up his notes then was escorted to the podium and began his presentation. Passing his fingers over his notes, he spoke with a continuous flow throughout his statements. "If you decide against Nye County, every issue of the infrastructure of the county will fail." He said the county would not be able to do its duty to protect the health and welfare of its citizens. In effect, he said that the federal government was trying to turn the county's status to that of a colony. "The United States has failed to cite a single case which upholds their theory."

At one point Marzulla asked that the map which the federal attorneys had displayed be placed on the easel again.

He said, "Judge, I am sure that *you* can see," and pointed to the map, while continuing his dissertation. This comment by a blind man drew a smile from the judge who grasped the humor of the moment.

When the attorneys concluded, Judge George told the courtroom, "What is being said is useful. Today we have had a magnificent civics class. This court will take the matter under advisement and render a decision within a week or so." He said that he served on a committee for the Justices of the Supreme Court and had traveled to the Soviet Union, at their request, to critique the Soviet Constitution. He stated that the U.S. Constitution was the oldest and best constitution in the world.

To illustrate that he would not be afraid to decide against the federal government, the judge told the audience, "President Truman decided to take control of the steel companies, but a judge, who had no more authority than I have, said he couldn't and the Supreme Court upheld him." The judge closed by saying the court would address the issue, would take the case under advisement and would deliver a decision as soon as possible, then declared adjournment.

Richard Carver and his supporters left the courtroom in smiles. Carver said, "I feel really good. The expression on the federal attorneys' faces showed me that we were winning."

Many people stood in the stifling desert heat along the shady side of the courthouse, as reporters took statements

The Battle of Jefferson Canyon

from the elated crowd. The attorneys for both sides agreed that this case would continue on to the Supreme Court. The ramifications of the courts' decision would be enormous. Huge federal payrolls and jobs were at stake. Responsibility and revenues derived from public lands could be suddenly shifted to the counties. The case was being watched, with interest, by an audience that reached across the nation.

Most of the people attending the hearing thought that Nye County was going to prevail. Many thought the judge's closing statements leaned in favor of Nye County. At any rate, there was a lot of confidence in Nye County's victory in the upcoming decision.

The decision did not come down quickly. The judge needed more information and asked for the parties to bolster their positions.

BOMB GOES OFF FOLLOWING JUDGE'S REQUEST

Early in August 1995, Judge LLoyd George asked the Department of Justice and Nye County to file additional briefs. He asked for additional documentation on "whether the state of Nevada does assert ownership."

The Nye County attorneys had a history of legislative backup. Ownership of the public lands was claimed in the "Sagebrush Bill" which was passed by the Nevada legislature in 1979. Later a joint resolution was passed unanimously in both houses in 1993 and unanimously again, with one legislator absent, in 1995. The resolutions state, "The State of Nevada has a strong moral claim upon the public land retained by the federal government." The resolution also had started a drive to remove the disclaimer clause to the public lands, made by the territorial legislature and contained in a preamble to the Nevada Constitution.

Hours after the judge asked for the briefs, on August 4, a forest supervisor's van was bombed in front of his home in Carson City, Nevada. Accusations are still flying as to who was responsible for the blast.

Nevada Senator Harry Reid blamed the county movement for stirring up trouble and implied that the bomber was part of that movement.

Nye County DA, Bob Beckett replied that there was no reason for anyone in the County Movement to do such a thing. He said the county's case was a good one and with such "great requests" coming from the judge, the county's position was getting more powerful each day.

It was hoped the bomber would be caught. Nye County posted a reward of one hundred thousand dollars for information leading to the arrest of the bomber. They were later ridiculed by the Forest Service state office for offering the reward and withdrew the offer. Meanwhile there was a call for a thorough investigation, even of possible federal involvement in the bombing.

For almost a month, the Nevada major media kept raising the point that someone involved in the county movement might be involved in the bombing. Previously, the major newspapers had ignored the Nye County battle even though it was going on right under their noses. It was evident whose side they were on.

MEDIA SCOFFS THEN SCRAMBLES

From the beginning, the position of the major newspapers was to ignore the County Movement. When Carver planned the road opening in Jefferson Canyon, a call was placed to the Las Vegas and Reno newspapers. A reporter at the *Reno Gazette Journal* said, "They can't open a road on federal land," and hung up on the caller. This exemplified how almost every newspaper in the country was treating the County Movement. Journalists from the environmental school of thought were deliberately keeping any County Movement news from being published. Even if it was news, they were not going to print anything that would help the counties.

Nevertheless, there were some editors who believed the public had the right to know what was really happening and printed the facts on every occasion. The champion of the counties was *The Livestock Market Digest*, edited by Lee Pitts and published by Chuck Stocks. This little paper had readers scattered throughout the West, and other publications asked it for reprint rights as the stories gained status. Lee Pitts wrote one particular story, *This Land is Our Land*, which was about the Carver Letter, and revealed a quicker understanding of the ideas than most attorneys demonstrate.

The *Elko Daily Free Press*, a major Northern Nevada paper, also featured the resistance move of the counties. The paper's editor, Dan Steninger, not only published stories, but wrote blistering editorials at every opportunity, slamming the federal officials for heavy-handed tactics.

The Battle of Jefferson Canyon

Local newspaper, the *Gateway Gazette* in Nye County, featured accounts of the organized revolt, doing a good job of reporting along with New Mexico's *Hatch Courier*.

Two more livestock publications, *The Nevada Rancher* and *The Cascade Cattleman* began running regular reports on the struggle between the counties and the feds.

But, the subject of the audacious counties remained taboo in most of the media, including Nevada television stations. Some said that Nevada's Governor and Attorney General pressured reporters to suppress news about the county revolt, but the rumor was never verified. The two did buy a lot of campaign space during elections.

The County Movement became the focus of national news after the Oklahoma City bombing in 1995 as the media tried to establish a link between the County Movement and the radical happenings across the nation. Carver was featured on the TV news magazine *48 Hours* in May of 1995. Reporters started falling over themselves, clamoring for interviews with the new folk hero of the West.

The *Reno Gazette Journal's* Sunday, August 13, 1995 edition carried the headline, "Suspicions linger for the County Movement. "The story subtly tried to put Richard Carver in bed with white supremacists, a completely unfounded rumor which was later debunked. The story also attempted to link other groups which the paper considered radical, including property rights advocates, with Carver and his supporters.

Conversely, the *Las Vegas Review Journal* Sunday paper had good, comprehensive stories about the issue, including the story about Eureka County Commissioners wanting to meet with Governor Miller on public land issues. The governor had ignored Eureka County's pleas for over a year. The county had completed studies on how the state could make money on managing the public lands and wanted to prove to Governor Miller, who publicly opposed state control of the lands, that the counties could do the job.

A related story in the same paper explained that the Ninth Circuit Court had allowed a suit for damages against the federal government to proceed. Victims of a 1987 Woodsford, California fire were suing the U.S, Forest Service and the Bureau on Land Management for more than $5 million dollars for losses incurred. The suit charged that negligence by federal employees had resulted in property losses. The story said that at first, a forest service employee could not find the fire. When it was finally located, the USFS sent a couple of fire fighters to put out a fire "about the size of a hood of a car." A pumper truck was dispatched, but only worked for five minutes and evidently broke down. Then, the USFS fire supervisor told the local volunteer fire department to stay away from the fire, because it was on federal land. In two hours the fire was totally out of control and ended up consuming several homeowners' holdings.

The Battle of Jefferson Canyon

So while, the Governor and the newspapers both advocated federal management, the media published stories of federal failure to cooperate and reported huge expenditures of the American taxpayer's money.

Meanwhile the County Movement suffered criticism, too.

When the bomb was detonated under the van at the Carson City home of Forest Supervisor Guy Pence, Senators Harry Reid and Richard Bryan both denounced the movement for "the irresponsible rhetoric that breeds violence." That crime remains a mystery. No one has been charged. Reid said the bomber was probably some radical from the dark underbelly of the County Movement.

Nye County's lead attorney, John Howard of the Individual Rights Foundation, was livid, saying, "Harry Reid is a coward for spouting libelous statements from his podium of Senate immunity."

The accusations had Carver's phone ringing constantly. Person after person called him, screaming about Reid's irresponsible statements. The Senator's comments drew a furious reaction from many people across the state. The Capitol Hill Boys were right about rhetoric causing people's blood to boil. Their rhetoric was doing just that, and the media was helping!

Three days later the *Reno News and Review*, a Reno tabloid paper featured Carver with a cover photo and a caption reading, "REBELS WITHOUT A CLUE, County Rule on the Road to Nowhere." The article, written by R. V. Scheide, talked about Scheide's hundred mile an hour motorcycle ride across a state with a 55 mile per hour speed limit to interview county and federal officials. Scheide even bragged about doing 115 miles an hour, in between talking about the lawlessness of the county movement. At that point in the story, Scheide says, "I am not going too fast, however to notice the continued absence of cattle. Yellow caution signs with black bull silhouettes continually warn this is open range territory, but aside from Carvers's small herd I've seen nary a steer. Just where the hell are the cowboys, let alone the cows? Where are the local customs and culture?"

The answer to R.V.'s question is that most of them were managed off the land by federal programs.

That story further said that Carver didn't let facts get in the way of his stories or ideas. The same might be said of the author of the story, who by the way, finished up his tale by gleefully running naked and howling across the same Nye County meadow, from which Wayne Hage's cattle had been removed from. Scheide had twisted many of his so-called facts and, not being up to speed on something besides his motorcycle, failed to talk about the real basis of Nye County's actions.

"Nye County's case," as attorney John Howard of the Individual Rights Foundation says, "is not about land. It is about the system."

The Battle of Jefferson Canyon

The most astounding media coverage for the County Movement came in the late fall of 1995. The October 23 issue of *Time* magazine hit the newsstands on October 18. There was not one issue to be found anywhere in Nevada within five days. The issue was bought off the stands just as rapidly all over the West. The cover story addressed the "Unrest in the West," giving Richard Carver and Nye County credit for being the leaders of a rebellion against federal rule. Carver and his wife, Midge, along with other Smokey Valley residents, are on the cover photo with the slogan DON'T TREAD ON ME emblazoned in red letters across Carver's chest.

The story tells how Carver was spurred to action and of his quest for support. The article dispels the idea of Carver being a white supremacist when it tells of the 18th century Carver family raising George Washington Carver, one of the most famous black men in history.

Time's story said that the dissatisfaction was no mere grumbling, but a real and concentrated resistance to federal control. This resistance was not armed with guns, but only with Carver's pocket rule book, the United States Constitution. The magazine managed to state the county's side of the argument better than any story by the national media, up to that time.

Carver and Nye County were now in the national spotlight. The feeding frenzy of television and newspaper reporters began all over, tying up Nye County's Courthouse telephones for days on end. The large state publications and television stations who had missed out on the Battle of Jefferson Canyon and ignored the continued fire building in Central Nevada, were now trying to catch up with the national media. To make matters tougher for them, they had to compete with some foreign correspondents, who were coming to America to report on the revolt.

Nye County had distanced itself from the radical fringe and had become a force to be reckoned with.

The Battle of Jefferson Canyon

NEVADA AG BOMBS NYE COUNTY

To clarify the state's position, Judge LLoyd George ordered the State of Nevada into the suit, *U.S.* vs. *Nye County* as a defendant on September 29, 1995. This action was in response to the DOJ naming the state as a defendant, along with Nye County. Many people said that the Nevada AG, Frankie Sue Del Papa was on the fed's side and would give away the state.

Del Papa was once considered for appointment as an Under Secretary of the Interior by Bruce Babbitt. Some people concluded that she would always align herself with the federal government because she was still had aspirations of attaining a federal post.

The state would presumably have to defend the Sagebrush Bill, claiming the public lands for the state, which had been on the books since 1979 but had never been implemented by any entity until Nye County, as a subdivision of the state, started asserting authority over the public lands.

Eureka County's Zane Miles asked the Nevada Legislative Committee on Public Lands to spur the state into a response, saying, "Would you want the executive branch (the Attorney General) to represent the legislature's interest in this matter?" Miles then offered the assistance of Eureka County, telling the committee, "Bill Schaeffer and I have already completed extensive research on this and we stand ready to help any way we can. "

Dean Rhoads, committee chairman, responded by saying he would look into the matter. Rhoads, a Nevada State Senator, had been a major force in legislating the Sagebrush Bill in 1979. In fact, Rhoads was sometimes called the father of the Sagebrush Rebellion, a title he wanted to live down. Although Dean had stood up to the onslaught of detractors' ridicule and flak from Washington at different times, he was now lukewarm on helping Nye County. It looked as though he wasn't going to line up to be run over again if he could help it.

However, there was clear legislative support for the county's position. Assemblyman, John Carpenter supported Nye County and had earlier even taken an entourage into the AG's office asking Del Papa to jump into the fray. He said at that time her reply was, "NO way." Now the AG had no choice but take a stand. When Carpenter was asked if the legislature would hire special counsel for the suit, he said, "We just don't have the horsepower to get it on." The legislature had just passed a resolution in 1995 proclaiming "Nevada has a strong moral claim to the public lands." Evidently it was immoral to defend that statement, because John could not get the legislative support for Nye County.

The Nevada Attorney General's first filing in response to Judge George's request was made on October 18, 1995, and asked for: 1. a judgment decreeing the nature of ownership and administrative authority of National Forest and other public lands within Nye County, 2.a judgement that ownership and jurisdiction are separate concepts, 3. that federal jurisdiction is nonexclusive, and 4. that the State of Nevada shares significant interest and jurisdiction on public lands. The AG also asked for judgement on the constitutionality of NRS 321 (the Sagebrush Bill) and Nye County Resolutions claiming all roads belonged to the county.

The Attorney General's press release said that Nye county had acted rashly when it bulldozed roads on Forest Service lands. Del Papa called the action, "the sort of behavior that tends to create problems and controversy and seldom solves anything." The AG also stated she believed very strongly that Nevada had a significant state interest and jurisdiction in public lands, but not an enforceable claim to title over the lands. She said, "The real fight for public land ownership is in Congress, not the courts." Then she added, "When the dust settles after this congressional session, there may be nothing left to fight about. The states may well end up with substantial ownership."

Nye County defense attorney, John Howard, publicly ripped Del Papa for not taking a forceful stance, while co-counsel, Roger Marzulla was pleased with her brief. Roger said the brief left the door open for Nye County to make its argument.

Then, as if realizing the door was open too wide, the Attorney General's office filed a subsequent brief on November 6, 1995 and left Nye County defenseless, with its pants down. In essence the State of Nevada failed to defend the Sagebrush Bill, agreed the federal government might own the land in question, and even refused to back the county on jurisdiction over roads. The Nevada Attorney General had finally taken the very path that Nye, Lander and Eureka Counties feared and stipulated away the state sovereignty.

The Nye County case was not the only one in which Del Papa sided with the feds.

It was later found out, that in the case of *New York vs. U.S.* Del Papa, who publicly opposed dumping nuclear waste in Nevada, had sided with the federal government on a similar issue in New York. In that case, the federal government was prevented form forcing New York to take adjacent states' low level nuclear waste, the very same action the federal government was trying to ram down Nevada's throat during Del Papa's term. Why would she want to force New York to submit to the very action she opposed in Nevada? New York won, but if the federal government had prevailed, would not that have set a precedent that Nevada might later be subject to?

Evidently Del Papa believed it was all right to take people's property without compensating them for it because she had also intervened *twice* with the federal government against Nevada citizen, Wayne Hage. First she sided with the feds on criminal charges, claiming damage to federal

The Battle of Jefferson Canyon

property, on a ditch controversy. Hage was cleaning his irrigation ditch right-of-way across USFS land. This was a right protected by Nevada State Law and was applicable to all lands *both* public and private. The Nevada Attorney General was attempting to implement an action which could nullify ditch easements all across the state, an action which directly conflicted with state law. Hage was found guilty, but the ruling was overturned by the appeals court.

Then Hage filed a multimillion dollar takings case against the federal government for taking his water and grazing rights which eventually forced him into bankruptcy.

Del Papa again intervened with the feds again by *hiring* an attorney who worked for an environmental group to plead the state's (or Del Papa's) view of the case against Hage. Hage was not only in a battle with the federal government, but also the government of his own state.

HAGE CLAIMS CASE GAINS STATUS

Wayne Hage had been dealt some severe setbacks in his conflicts with the USFS. Wayne thought he was right and stood by his guns. The gutty rancher wrestled with the bureaucrats to a point that most people would not consider prudent. Federal actions had virtually taken away the basis of his ranching operation, grass and water. Many contend that Wayne's book *Storm Over Rangelands* was the reason for this federal vendetta. You just don't say the federal government is power-hungry and wrong.

Following the confiscation of his cattle in 1991 and the denying of access to his range, Wayne filed suit claiming damages for taking away his ranch and his livelihood. The case dragged for years and cost thousands of dollars. Wayne was again bucking up against both the federal and state attorney generals. Every time a hearing date was set, it would be postponed. Wayne had principals but he was paying a terrific cost to defend them. But after dragging for a while, the case of *Hage vs. U.S.* suddenly began to look as thought Hage had some serious standing in the court. Finally on February 1, 1996, Hage received an order from the U.S. Court of Federal Claims Chief Judge, Loren Smith, recognizing that Hage's rights to water and grazing may preempt those of the United States Forest Service.

The one page order said that the court would hold a limited evidentiary hearing addressing Hage's property interest as defined by Nevada law in water rights, ditch rights-of-way and forage rights in the Toiyabe National Forest.

The Battle of Jefferson Canyon

The order said, "The court concludes that a limited evidentiary hearing is necessary to the court's analysis of plaintiffs' takings claims. Plaintiffs (Hages) claim vested water rights encompassing vested ditch rights of way and forage rights from the mid 1800's. Defendant (USFS) claims the same water rights beginning the 1900's. If plaintiffs can prove that their water rights vested before the defendant claimed its water rights, plaintiffs' water rights precede defendant's water rights. Therefore, under the prior appropriation doctrine, plaintiffs would have priority water rights. If plaintiffs prove prior vested rights in the water encompassing forage rights of way, plaintiffs are entitled to proceed with their taking claim."

The document goes on to say, "Defendant (USFS) claims that plaintiffs do not have conclusive water rights until completion of the state adjudication procedure. Furthermore, even if plaintiffs do have water rights, defendant claims that those rights would not permit ingress and egress of the livestock to the water. Following defendant's theory through to its logical conclusion, defendant believes the court should rule that even if the plaintiffs owned property rights dating from the 1800's, such water and ditch rights have no relevance today because of state administrative proceedings and the application of federal law."

The final paragraph reads, "Contrary to the defendant's (USFS) position, this court concludes that if the plaintiff's predecessors in interest had property rights in the 1880's, the rights presumptively still exist. It is the court's duty to determine whether the plaintiffs have the property rights at issue, the scope of those rights, and whether the government action with respect to those rights requires compensation under the Fifth Amendment."

The order then set up a telephone conference, to discuss the issues of the limited evidentiary hearing.

The Hages had completed extensive research into their property rights, which are the focus of this case. They claimed they had a clear chain of title to the rights that would be hard to knock down.

Under Nevada water law the basic rule proving beneficial use of water was livestock watering. Range and stock water were property rights. According to Hage, the Bureau of Land Management's and USFS's legitimate job was to create allotments which were a recognition of property rights to water and forage.

Another case, which may have some bearing on Hages is one decided in 1957, *Ansolobere vs. Laborde*. In this case, one rancher tried to take over a neighbor's range through a claim to water rights that both were using on that range. Although the court decision declared that the Taylor Grazing Act had the right to adjudicate the range, its findings held that beneficial use of the water rights consisted of livestock foraging on the range, and the two could not be separated. If this doctrine continues through the Hage case, it will solidify many claims to grazing across the west. The federal government may have to start paying for the grazing reductions and cancellations they have been implementing. It will also solidify the rights of and lift the federal regulatory burden from all other users of the public domain.

Eureka County considered filing for intervener status in the Hage Case, claiming the grazing reductions in their county have drastically reduced tax revenues from the livestock industry. They planned to ask for personal property tax monies the county had not received because of federal pressure to reduce grazing.

Another player who would be heard from in a similar suit was Hage's neighbor, Steve Wilmans, of the RO Ranch in Smokey Valley, who also has water rights on a range that the Forest Service traded to a mining company. The trade was completed without compensating Wilmans for the properties.

On March 8, 1996, the claims court judge issued an opinion in the Hage case partially granting a motion for summary judgement made by the federal government. Stipulating that there would be an additional limited evidentiary hearing, the judges' findings included some eye-opening statements; "If Nevada Law recognized the right to graze cattle near bordering water as part of a vested water right before 1907, when Congress created the Toiyabe National Forest, plaintiffs may have a right to the forage adjacent to their alleged water rights on the rangeland." The judge had solidified his February ideas of the mechanics of the use of range and water.

The judge also stated, "When the federal government created the Toiyabe National Forest, it could not unilaterally ignore private property rights on the public domain. If Congress wanted to remove all property interests in the public domain which were created by the state under state law, the Constitution would have required the federal government to pay just compensation." It sounded like the Hages had a very strong case against the government. Many people, environmentalists and ranchers alike, were watching this case with interest. Rancher's rights were hanging by threads which this case could turn into hawsers if Hages prevailed. In fact, this case could be the major stepping stone for reduction of federal control, unless the government wants to pay for that control in the 17 Western States.

The other rights of access to the rangelands are protected by the same state statutes which protect grazing and water rights. Grazing is only a part of the split estate that has been established over lands in the West. Many of the present restrictions on access to the public lands for mining, camping and woodgathering would be mitigated by a return to state law.

According to Zane Miles, the Nevada Territorial Legislature had enacted laws recognizing grazing rights, laws assimilated into state law and never repealed. Then

The Battle of Jefferson Canyon

Miles says, two years after statehood, the state legislature enacted laws recognizing the right to mine   on the rangeland. The legislature reaffirmed the multiple use concept, preventing any one user from locking others from the rangeland. The multiple use concept was initially the goal of the federal land management laws. The laws were later ignored and more single use concepts begun to be implemented, such as attempting to convert to only fishing, hunting and recreation by planting nonnative animals and fish then designating protection areas and essentially zoning out grazing, mining and timbering.

JUDGE RULES AGAINST NYE COUNTY, PARTIALLY

While the Hage case was making headyway, Nye County was losing ground. A court decision was about to take the wind out of the rebels' sails. The final hearing in the *U.S. vs. Nye County* case was held in the courtroom of Judge Lloyd George March 7, 1995.

The Las Vegas court filled with spectators, some from adjacent states, to witness the final round in this suit which had been going on for almost a year. Judge George commended the people attending the hearing, saying that the courtrooms and congress were the proper forums in which to settle disputes. The judge's opinion followed one week later, as promised in his statements in the court.

The judge had asked for additional briefs on the relationship of the Nye County suit to the case, Scott vs. Lattig, which addressed the power of the federal government to dispose of public lands. This case concerned an island in the Snake River, over which two individuals had claimed title. This case hinged on whether the acquisition of the island through the federal land office was valid and if the land office had proper title to begin with.

Judge LLoyd George ruled in favor of the federal government in the case on one count and partially on another of the five counts against Nye County. He found in favor of the federal government in the dispute over ownership and management of the public lands and partially in their favor on the enforcement of resolutions.

The Battle of Jefferson Canyon

The judge said that he had read the amicus briefs of Lander, White Pine, and Eureka Counties and despite their claims, the ownership issue had already been decided by numerous court decisions.

The major newspapers and the federal government claimed the ruling to be a major blow to the Second Sagebrush Rebellion which had sprung up across the West. However, Nye County also claimed a win because the judge said there was shared jurisdiction on the public lands, a fact the federal management agencies had been ignoring in the past.

Zane Miles was not happy with the way the case had been argued. He said, "The Department of Justice did not win this case, Nye County threw it away." Miles said, "I have had it with amicus briefs. They are worthless because you can't get up and defend your own position." Miles said that appeal on the Nye case would be impossible because points that should have been part of the case were not brought forward and, consequently, could not be used in an appeal.

According to Miles, the denial of intervenor status for Eureka County was due to a stipulation made by John Howard early on. Zane said he did not fault Howard for this, because he had to make a quick decision at the time. John Howard was also blamed for a time frame stipulation in November that threw a bump in the road.

In 1995 John Howard had hired Roger Marzulla to assist him in the defense of Nye County, but in the following months disagreements over tactics created a rift between the two. Both attorneys complained that the other filed papers without proper consultation.

In the final moments of the trial, John Howard was relieved of his duties and Roger Marzulla became lead counsel. Because the Nevada AG had opted to sell Nye County down the river, Marzulla and Carver did not think they would win the case and wanted to salvage whatever they could for the county. So shared jurisdiction was the route taken. This was much the same banner that Catron County, New Mexico had been marching under.

In the courtroom argument, Marzulla said that the Constitution had been formulated to protect the people from the very dominance over 93% of Nye County that the federal government was asserting. Marzulla said, "The heart of the matter is what authority the federal government has over the public lands and what authority the state has."

Marzulla said that even if the federal government owned the land, ownership was not jurisdiction. He asserted that giving the federal government what they wanted "would tilt the fragile balance between state and federal authority." He also said that exclusive federal jurisdiction would be an excessive concentration of authority in one entity.

The Nevada Deputy Attorney General, Wayne Howell, made one small statement in defense of jurisdiction. "The State of Nevada has some jurisdiction over public lands and we want to ensure that is maintained." The state's final brief did not defend the Nevada Legislature's 1995 resolutions regarding claims to the public lands or the 1979 Sagebrush Bill, which Nye County had earlier relied on for their defense.

After the hearing, Nye County District Attorney Bob Beckett said that he had previously disagreed with the direction the defense was taking in the case. He and some others had advocated going for broke on the ownership issue, but now agrees that concept would not have won, given the direction the court was heading. Beckett said, "The good thing is that the judge said the jurisdiction and management of the public lands has to be shared, until the supremacy clause kicks in."

The judge refused to rule on the "scope and constitutionality of legislation in advance of its immediate adverse effect in the context of a concrete case."

In the end, the judge ruled that "Nevada undoubtedly retains jurisdiction over the federal lands, but Congress equally surely retains the power to enact legislation respecting those lands." The findings state that the suit was not the appropriate vehicle to define the broad boundaries between local and federal jurisdiction.

Dick Carver, although keeping a positive spin on the decision, was still somewhat stunned with the court's findings. Carver had expected to lose the case in the lower courts but had still believed that the Constitution would support his beliefs. He had been hoping for the judge to sustain the views of the framers of the Constitution and was disappointed that the judge failed to do so. But, Dick said the decision was not as hard on the county as first impressions led some to believe. Carver said, "I think we came out smelling like a rose. We are not losing, because the feds are out here trying to work with us. This dispute would have never occurred if they had cooperated three years ago."

In the previous two months, the agencies had begun making special efforts through meetings with Nye County, trying to find consensus on land management matters. Meetings for this purpose had been unheard of before this time.

Carver confessed that the county's position became hard to uphold, "With the State Attorney General not defending state laws, there was nothing we could do." The Nevada AG's submissive approach to the issue was a major disappointment to many people who commented on the hearing.

The disappointment with the state's stand came from more than just one direction. Not only was the Nevada Attorney General, Frankie Sue Del Papa handing Nye County over to the wolves, she had hired special counsel, Thomas Lustig of the National Wildlife Federation, to represent Nevada *opposing* Wayne Hage in his takings claim against the federal government! Many people are screaming foul at this point. Should someone in the state AG's office be assisting in a federal action, which was taking a citizens property rights?

The two attorneys who had done the most research on equal footing and jurisdiction, Bill Schaeffer and Zane Miles, ended up with the smallest voices in the case. This was a disappointing and frustrating role for the pair, who had committed countless hours of time and effort to establish a basis for comprehensive arguments. They needed to go down swinging, not be relegated to the corner and left holding the towel.

If the case had been better managed, would the outcome have been different? This a point which would be argued time and again. Some charges against Nye County, including the jurisdiction over roads were dropped by the DOJ. However, it appears the judge had listened to earlier Nye County arguments. In reading the judge's findings, it looked as though he tried to touch on all the legal theories presented in his court. This included equal footing, the question of whether the states acquired title to the public lands at statehood, and Constitutional authority. He did say the original thirteen states did not acquire their dry lands as a public trust, to hold in common for all the people.

Rather, the states could and did pass ownership of the unappropriated dry lands to private individuals to the exclusion of the people in common. Does this imply the western states should have had the same opportunity?

It looked as though the dispute would continue, even though the federal government saw the court ruling as an end to the controversy. Whether Arizona, who was planning on intervening, would appeal the case or bring a new suit forward would remain to be seen.

Nothing was settled in the eyes of the rural people. The judge did not rule on the constitutionallity of: the Nevada statehood act, or the federal government's ability to own lands not falling within the enclave designation. In essence the whole case left the core of issues brought in by Nye County unresolved.

But, the fracas did get the attention of congress. Just what in the hell was going on out West?

The Battle of Jefferson Canyon

RURAL COUNTIES GET CONGRESSIONAL EAR

One of the allies in the continuing battle, Eureka County would continue its fight for control and take advantage of the opportunity laid at their feet.

Senator Ted Stevens of Alaska sent two men west to gather information on the "unrest in the West." Stevens was the chairman of the Committee on Government Affairs and had his team investigating the reason for the troubled relationship between federal and local governments.

The first stop on their tour was the Las Vegas, Nevada final hearing of the Nye County Suit on March 7, 1996. The team was next scheduled to visit Graham County, Arizona the following day to look into its problems on the Gila River road crossing, discussed in an earlier chapter.

So they could gather first hand knowledge of the issues, the men scheduled a meeting with county representatives after the hearing in Las Vegas. The two were swamped with allegations of federal misuse of power, twisting of facts by federal employees, failure to adhere to federal laws and rules, and arbitrary federal decision making. The allegations would be substantiated in a hearing later in the month in Washington, D.C.

At that time, Eureka County, Nevada representatives were scheduled to meet with Paul Stockler, Special Counsel for the Government Affairs Committee and deliver the facts on federal malfeasance that had been gathered. John Balliette, Eureka County Resource Manager had court decisions as evidence.

One case in particular involved the Filippini family of Battle Mountain, Nevada, who had been moved off their range through BLM management decisions made with what the judge said were skewed data and failure to follow proper procedure. The person doing the range evaluation was inexperienced, lost and not on the Filippini range that was to be affected by the decisions. Completely unfounded and unsupportable data was gathered by the BLM. The appeals judge ruled in favor of the Filippinis, setting aside the BLM's full force and effect decision rendered against them.

Despite the judge's ruling, The Battle Mountain District of the BLM ignored the decision and proceeded to do business as usual. The agency said the judge was inexperienced and did not know what he was doing. If the decision had been against the rancher, could he have ignored the ruling?

The suit had cost the Filippini's thousands of dollars in attorney fees, contesting the arbitrary decisions made by BLM District Manager, Wayne King.

In a humorous aside, the Nevada Alliance for Public Lands (a group formed by members of county public land advisory commission members) later sent King an award along with a mirror. The award was for, "Being the Most

The Battle of Jefferson Canyon

Arbitrary and Capricious Land Manager of the Year." The mirror was an attempt to get the man to look at himself while making his decisions. Upon receiving the award, it was rumored that King first laughed then, after a bit of thought threw a dirt fit, cussing and throwing papers around his office.

Arbitrary decision making would be just one of many problems associated public lands grazing issues. With the Rangeland Reform now being implemented, there was evidence that the new advisory committees were not knowledgeable enough to do a proper job.

Balliette told the Washington investigators that he did not believe that the majority of the people on the newly appointed Rangeland Advisory Councils had any knowledge of the laws and procedures they were supposed to follow. "In fact," John says, "there is a blatant disregard of law and procedure by the RAC's. It is scary to think that one of these councils is making policy for 60,000 people and they don't know anything about the laws they have to follow or about natural resource management." Three or four training sessions could not provide the amount of knowledge needed to make informed decisions, according to John. Balliette said that the RAC meetings had been poorly attended with only three or four interested public involved.

He thought this was poor showing of true grass roots input, which the reform package was supposed to establish.

Balliette did maintain, however, that there were Resource Management Plans in place and that, as a whole, most of them were quite good. The problem was, that they were not always being followed and sometimes could not be found in some of the federal land management offices. As an example, when Balliette asked the Caliente, Nevada B.L.M. office for a copy, the officials didn't know if they had one. The document was finally found in storage, in a warehouse out back. Another rulebook was being ignored by the feds.

By the time they finished with their fact gathering, the Special Counsel for Committee on Government Affairs would have a mountain of data for their committeemen Met Johnson alerted the Western States Coalition to dig up all the facts available on the matter.

Whether Congress planned on reining in some of the agencies or enacting some relief legislation was not known. The west was ready to document the injuries.

Eureka and other central Nevada Counties were planning to ask all who would listen for a pilot project, allowing local management of the public lands. They said the federal management was costing the American taxpayers far too much and it was time to bring some common sense into the picture.

The Battle of Jefferson Canyon

Despite what some environmental groups were saying about rancher welfare, most of the land management budget went for top-heavy government administration costs. In fact, the more than 500 million spent by the federal government was going mostly for paperwork, administration and recreation programs. It was primarily a program of federal bureaucratic welfare.

If ranchers had to pay for use of previously established rights to water and forage, should recreationists be allowed free use? Federal land use fees for public use of county maintained airstrips, gravel pits used for county roads, and other community uses for public lands were already being implemented. A toll gate was being erected where everyone would eventually have to pay to access the public domain. The federal government had been running short of funds and would begin to look at every aspect to gain revenue for their agencies.

THE FIGHT CONTINUES

Despite court decisions saying the Bureau of Land Management's Battle Mountain, Nevada office was skewing data and using bad range assessment practices, that office would continue its vicious vendetta against the Filippini family.

During a meeting in Austin, Nevada, several people have said that BLM representative Jerry Smith shocked the group with a statement about the Filippinis case, which was undergoing an appeal by the BLM.

When Smith was asked about the court expense to the American taxpayer and to the Filippinis, he said that they (The audience) should not worry about the Fillippinis, they had a lot of money and would survive all right. (Is there jealousy among federal bureaucrats because some people have hard earned money and holdings that the government workers do not have?) He also reiterated that the judge was too young and inexperienced to properly judge the case.

Met Johnson's Western States Coalition had requested United States Attorney General Janet Reno investigate the Forest Service in Utah, after it was proven the agency had used the same arbitrary practices and decision against the Boulder Mountain, Utah permittees as the BLM had against the Filippinis. The Inspector General started its internal investigation of that Department of Agriculture sub-bureau, the US Forest Service in early 1996.

The Battle of Jefferson Canyon

Arizona representative, Joe Hart said he was pushing for the Arizona Constitutional Defense Council to take the issues of Equal Footing and ownership of the public lands directly to the Supreme Court. Joe said he had a lot of support for the action and had a commitment from 11 western states to join if Arizona took the lead. Joe said that when the Nevada Attorney General shot Nye County in the back, there wasn't any way for Arizona to help. Arizona's Constitutional Defense Council had voted to intervene in the *U.S. vs. Nye County* suit but funding was blocked by the Arizona Attorney General , who controlled the funds. The Arizona legislature was working on giving the CDC total autonomy on decisions regarding proposed actions when the judge's decision against Nye County came down. The new bill was passed by the legislature and awaiting the governor's promised signature at publication date. Arizona would soon be mustering forces for an assault of its own.

Karen Budd-Falen's father-in-law John Falen of Orovada, Nevada had been awarded more than $80,000 in attorney fees he had to pay to defend his rights against an arbitrary decision by federal land managers on a range issue. This was truly a first in this area and the Budd-Falen law offices forged it out.

Karen Budd was beginning to mark wins on the scoreboard. She was quoted in a January, 1996, *Denver Post* article on the Sagebrush Rebellion, "The tide is changing, and if you do another survey in another five years, you'll see a lot more wins on our side."

The Hage case would probably become a landmark decision when it was it was finally rendered. Wayne's takings claim would be the focus of the ensuing months.

While all the main skirmishes were already in progress, the armorers for states rights found another tactical weapon and were preparing it for use. This new offense could well come from the research and theories of another lady attorney, Lana Marcussen of Albuquerque, New Mexico. Lana's theory was that reservations made after statehood were invalid under the Constitution. Some of those reservations may include Forest Reserves, Indian reservations and perpetual reservation of the public lands by the 1976 Federal Land Management Policy Act. (These were the lands held in trust for final disposal in most of the statehood acts.)

In July of 1995, Lana had already won some bets with New Mexico attorneys when the New Mexico State Supreme Court said that the governor could not make gaming agreements favoring Indians, even after the agreements had been verified by the Bureau of Indian Affairs. At that time the New Mexico Attorney General was in a quandry, whether to shut down Indian casinos or open up gaming statewide. Early in 1996, The U.S. Supreme Court ruled likewise that Indian tribes could not go to federal courts to force states into agreements allowing Indian Gaming.

The Battle of Jefferson Canyon

Lana claimed that this could be the beginning of the end of the Bureau of Indian Affairs. Indians may finally be able to own their land instead on occupying a federal reservation. In the long run the Indians may be better off.

The November 28, 1994 issue of *U.S. News & World Report* called the BIA, "The Worst Federal Agency," and told some amazing facts: The article said the agency's accounting system was such a mess that inspectors could not perform an audit on $3.2 billion of $4.4 billion in BIA assets. The Indian Trust Fund has been unable to reconcile accounts, now amounting to $2.1 billion, for more than a hundred years. The story also said little of the agency's money was finding its way to the people who needed it.

Like the Indians, contracts had been made with the other people of the West. Contracts with states and individuals who relied on the contracts for economic base and livelihood. Like the Indians, those contracts and trusts were being broken, both by Congress and the federal agencies. Would there ever be equitable settlement?

Nothing was settled in the eyes of the rural people. The judge in the Nye County suit did not rule on the constitutionality of the statehood act which forced the state to disclaim the public lands, or the federal government's ability to own lands not falling within the enclave designation of Article 1, Sec 8 of the Constitution. In essence, the whole case left the core of issues brought in by Nye County unresolved.

During the last week of April, 1996, Dick Carver and Cameron McRae spent time in Washington D.C. talking with Congressmen and agency heads about the problems between the federal and local governments. They thought it would be beneficial to show the people on the hill what Nye County stood for and set themselves aside from radical elements such as the militias and the white supremacists that had been dominating much of the news at that time. The commissioners wanted people to know that Nye County was carrying its fight through the courts and politically, rejecting any armed method of resistance.

During this period a group of People in Montana who called themselves the Montana Militia had charges filed against them by the Department of Justice and were surrounded in a ranch compound by the FBI. Members of the group claimed "sovereignty" and said they did not have to procure drivers licenses, pay county taxes and were only subject to a common law court, which they had established. It was reported that some had declared U.S. currency improper money and then issued worthless checks. Some had defaulted on their farm loans, lost their holdings, then declared the loan agreements were not valid because the federal government did not have the power to make the loans. Others had threatened elected officials and denied the authority of just about every government entity in their state.

The Battle of Jefferson Canyon

Carver said that actions such as these were giving the people who were taking the proper path a black eye. He darn sure did not advocate the threatening of a county official and he never would. Carver had proved he did not like threats to county officials coming from anyone, including the federal government.

In Washinton D.C., Carver and company were met with a cool reception in the Department of Justice and found out that it had been rumored in the agency that Carver was planning another road opening. Carver was told by Carolyn Zander, one of the DOJ attorneys at the Las Vegas Trial, that there was a difference between jurisdiction and management. over the public lands. Carver disputed this, saying, "Didn't you agree with the judge at the trial that there was shared management and jurisdition?" He said that Zander agreed. It looked as though the federal agencies might be headed back to their old habits of trying to dominate the public lands.

However, Carver and County Manager Les Bradshaw were met with a warm reception in the Pentagon where they met with heads of the Air Force which was asking for reauthorization of another 15 year land set aside for the Nellis Bombing Range in Nye County. Everyone was excited when Carver and Bradshaw walked into the room. Prenotified of the meeting, one of the Air Force personell took an issue of the *Time Magazine* containing the Nye

County story, ran the cover across a color copy machine. The employees then had Carver autograph many copies. One high ranking air force officer said that Carver was his hero and he thought that Nye County's challenge of federal power was justified and needed.

When Nye County met with the head of the USFS, Jack Ward Thomas and four of his staff, the agency offered to cooperate and listened to McRae attentively when he talked about the issues. He and Carver both talked about the lack of communication and the loss of trust. When Carver was asked what he thought about establishing some guidelines, he said, "We are not going to sign any MOU (memorandum of understanding) then have it put on the shelf like what happened to Catron County, New Mexico. We want a protocol agreement such as we now have with your sister agency, the Department of Energy for the Yucca Mountain Nuclear Waste Project."

The protocol he was referring to had been drawn up and agreed upon by both Nye County and the DOE and was signed by the top person, Secretary Hazel O'Leary. Protocol means everyone will work together on *all* issues. The document is a list of procedures which must be used when changes in approved plans are made or new plans are being contemplated. According to Carver, Nye County had problems with matters on the project only one time that Nye had to invoke the protocol. Otherwise, the department and the county had consulted and came to agreements on a steady basis.

The Battle of Jefferson Canyon

Carver said that Thomas was agreeable about the use of such a document and seemed ready to work with the county. Dick quoted Thomas as saying, "I'm not concerned about the Nye County law suit. I knew how the judge would decide. I *am* concerned about what brought the law suit on." Carver thought that Thomas was going to help solve the differences between the Forest Service and Nye County.

Carver was pleased with the meeting with the Forest Service but a bit disappointed with the lukewarm reception in the Department of the Interior.

Carver had still hoped to meet with Bruce Babbitt but Babbitt was out of town. Carver and McRae did meet with Assistant Secretary of the Interior, Bob Armstrong and four of his staff. When the Interior officials mentioned the Filippini case, Carver said, "Issues like the Filippini case were not helping to build trust with federal agencies."

Now the War on the West is broadening according to Cheryl Johnson, President of the New Hampshire Landowners Alliance. In a May 1996 article written for the *People for the West* publication, she said, "It's not a case of East against West--it's the government against everyone! The preservationists want to lock up the whole country--not just the West." Johnson said that the people of New Hampshire's livelihoods were not threatened by grazing, mining and water rights issues but by Wild and Scenic rivers designations, which were infringing on private property rights.

Her parting words were, "The next time you hear the phrase, 'War on the West,' don't be tempted to think that it's East against West. We are with you, not against you. We are actually fighting the 'War on America!'"

The war may be perceived as the federal government against everyone, but it was turning into a battle between the urban and rural ideals. Urban preservationists had carried out a terrificly successful political campaign, aided by the federal bureaucracies, which had already made a serious dent in the rural way of life. Many of the country people resented the preservationists, who had failed miserably in maintaining a decent way of life in their own urban neighborhoods, taking a major role in directing what happened in the rural areas. It was especially resented when the pressure came from those who did not have sufficient knowledge to help make the proper decisions. The rural people felt they knew the country best and they just may, because they had lived a lifetime of experiences in their region. They didn't want their country *or* their livelihoods destroyed.

In 1990, Northern Arizona University School of Forestry Dean, Dr. Wallace Covington, expressed great concern about declining forest vitality. He said that there was only a thirty-year window remaining to establish pre-European settlement conditions in our forests and after that there may be no reclamation of forest health for untold years. Dr.Covington's colleague, Dr. Dave Garret former head of

The Battle of Jefferson Canyon

the Ecology Department of the same school, recently completed a study of the forest conditions of Eastern Arizona and said, "The forest will become increasingly diseased, insect infested, die and then burn." If this was true, there wasn't much time to quit quibbling and start to work.

In late April and early May of 1996, the Southwest was experiencing a prolonged drought which had left the forests dry as tinder. Huge forest fires had already broken out and summer hadn't begun. That huge fuel load that scientists had warned was building up in the timber began to show its ugly, dangerous presence. The mass devastation was needless, according to some natural resource scientists. Thoughtful timber harvesting and grazing could greatly reduce that fuel load.

The Sierra Club had been calling for a total ban on commercial harvesting. Would the preservationists soon have to choose between walking around a few stumps and cow manure pies in a healthy forest or wading through ankle-deep ash over an area that looked as though it has had a nuclear bomb dropped on it? They could go visit another forest and leave the burned forest to the scorched remaining residents.

Enlightened former Earth Firster, Howard Hutchinson vehemently believed some good decisions could be made if everyone had the proper knowledge. Howard said, "It is time for those of us who really care about the environment to recognize that the primary threat (to forest health) is not commercial interests but the misguided organizations whose objectives are fund raising via false propaganda and scare tactics. Considering the dry conditions leading into this year's fire season, we may be too late for many of our forests." Hutchinson also said it was time to let the people who knew the land best have the major role in management decision making.

Dick Carver agreed and said that the decisions could be made faster *and* better closer to home.

In the spring of 1996, Dick Carver was still filling numerous speaking engagements across the country and continuing to build support for a greater county role in government relationships. Carver had said many times that the battle would have to be carried politically as well as through the courts. At this time, he was not the only soldier in the front lines because now a burgeoning army of support for the states rights movement was springing up across America. Carver, who now called the United States Constitution the "Rulebook for America," was still out telling everyone who would listen, one of the basics that Bruce Babbitt taught him . . .

When you think you are right....*never, ever give up.*

It looked like it was going to be a long, hard fought war.

The Battle of Jefferson Canyon

Index

Miles, Zane 53-57, 60, 65, 72, 119-120, 138, 147-148, 150, 154
Miller, Bob 36, 71, 116, 133-134
Nicholson, Rachael 90
O'Leary, Hazel 168
Pence, Guy 134
Perry, James
Pitts, Lee 18, 21, 77, 96, 131
Presley, Ed 22-25, 27, 32-33, 35, 49, 51, 64-65, 83, 92
Reid, Harry 129, 134
Reno, Janet 106-107, 117, 119
Rhoads, Dean 44, 139
Schaeffer, William 53, 56-57, 59-60, 72, 119-120, 123, 138, 154
Scheide, R.V. 135
Schweikert, Dave 63
Shrimp, Ron 51
Skelton, Roberta 51
Sloan, Jim 15
Smith, Marshall 58
Smith, Bert 34
Smith, Jerry 162
Smith, Loren 143
Spiller, Sam 111-112
Spring, Kelly 105-106
Steninger, Dan 131
Stevens, Ted 156
Stockler, Paul 156
Stocks, Chuck 131
Strickland, Rose 44
Stringer, Jim 49, 106-108
Symington, Fife 40, 66-67, 99, 113

The Battle of Jefferson Canyon